Whispers

Just Before Dawn

An Inspiring Anthology of Poems, Letters, and Essays

Volume I

By

Chuck Goode

Published by Goode God Publishing

MMXIII

Copyright 2013 by Chuck Goode

Library of Congress Control Number: 1-1008613041

ISBN: 978-0-9912166-0-4

Forward

I lay there, unable to sleep. My mind racing, my thoughts lacking form or direction, I did my best to take control of the moment and will my dancing thoughts to form an idea. After all, I am the Renaissance man. God has blessed me with the ability to create a plan to remedy whatever obstacle I am confronted with. I knew I could do this, and do it well. But now, there I was, just hours before I needed to present what was the most important creative writing of my life, to date, lying there, my thoughts scattering like light dry snowflakes at the hint of a breeze. Words just seemed to dance one imagining beyond my creative grasp, like a dollar bill that falls to the ground on a windy day in March.

My poem was to be the tribute from my extended family that would be printed on the back page of the funeral bulletin to represent our loving sentiments for our matriarch, my grandmother, Theresa Fauntroy Cohen. I had dread this day for what seemed my entire life, and had rehearsed in my mind a thousand times all the beautiful things I wanted to say about her. Now the moment was here and no words I could bring to mind seemed adequate to express what I felt in my heart.

I had prayed that the Holy Spirit would use me to bless my family and all those that knew her, but the words did not come. I would like to say I got up and took pen in hand as an act of faith, believing that my prayer would be answered if I took that one little step, but it was more an act of desperation. I figured that if I just put a few words to paper the rest would eventually come. As soon as I began to write, the words just flowed from my pen. They came as fast as I could write them, and I knew that they were not my own. "A pink rose bloomed on a red rose vine...." (*'In the Fullness of my Time'*)

Since that early morning, I have had many such challenges, and

He has never failed me. In fact, I have come to know that when my creativity seems to betray me, there is something very special coming; just before dawn.

In my unenlightened days, I considered those buzzer beater experiences as proof that I worked better under pressure. It was an ability I brought to the table. I have since reflected on other instances when the words just seemed to come, and understand that in those days I had been just too spiritually disconnected to see the hand of God in my writing.

Now that I am fully aware of where my creativity comes from, it is not unusual for me to be awakened out of my sleep with a strong urging to go to my quiet place and just listen for a few moments. I don't hear voices, but I hear direction in my spirit of what I am to write. I am sure it is in these moments that God 'supercharges' the gift He has given me to say something that will inspire or encourage someone.

That's why I named my publishing company Goode God. It is my way of acknowledging that He is the one who gives me the very best of my creative capabilities.

This anthology shares many of those creations born in His mind and given to me to put on paper. Those creations address all aspects of life, but share one common thread: the love of God. I am so blessed that He has chosen me to be a vessel through whom His blessing of encouragement can flow during this trying season. I pray that something in these pages blesses you. I pray that I will always have the heart to listen to those whispers, just before dawn.

Dedication

This book is dedicated to all of the loving souls the Lord has blessed me with to share my journey down the road of life. You have encouraged me as much as you have inspired me.

To all of those that have gone on before me; My mother, Yvonne Cohen Goode Satterfield; my father, Thomas "Buck" Goode; my stepfather, John "Jay" Satterfield; my grandmother, Theresa Fauntroy Cohen; my grandfather, George Washington Cohen; my aunts and uncles, especially Magnolia Goode and Delmore Goode; all my cousins and friends, especially my brother from another mother, Albie Reaves, who was the best of both. I pray that your legacy of love will be immortalized by what you have inspired me to share.

To all of those who still walk locked step with me on this pathway through life, and who have in some way counseled, encouraged, or inspired me: my wife, Cleta; my children, Tamika and Trevor and their mates Chamar and Josette; my stepchildren Robyn and Paul; and my grandchildren, Channing, Chris, Nick, Umberto, Anari, Nico, Chunel, Christian, Jacylah (LaLa), and Braylon (BD); my sister Terrie Goode; her son Chris Wright; his wife Mari and their daughter Madison Yvonne; my special brothers Moe and Larry Polite; our special sisters and brothers, my nieces, my nephews, and my 3 living aunts, my mother's sisters who call me son, Lucy Green, Nellie Wright, and Lillian Polite. You are the wealth I have stored upon this earth. May you be blessed by the words that fill these pages, and know that you have been an inspiration, and have had a profound influence on what I write and the life I live.

To my spiritual teachers, Pastor James C. Jones, Pastor Raymond M. Gordon, Bishop LeRoi Bailey, Bishop Courtney McBath, and Bishop Kim W. Brown: thank you for being vessels of wisdom.

A Special Dedication

Sometimes in life we find ourselves in a special situation that requires special prayer to get us through. Often God uses ordinary people to do unexpected and extraordinary things to answer us. My brother, Michael "Moe" Polite was used by God to lift me from such a situation. I thank him for being a yielded vessel. I praise God for him. May his life be filled with extraordinary blessings.

Thank You Brother Moe for Being There

Thank you Bro for being there;

a tool in God's strong hand.

We know our help comes from The Lord,

but is delivered man to man.

He uses ordinary people

to administer His grace;

A shining light, a helpful hand,

A loving heart, a familiar face.

I am thankful that He chose you,

And that you saw fit to care,

I thank Him that His word is true;

I thank Him that you were there

What's Going On?

The first time I can remember 'waking up with a song in my heart', as I used to call it, was the morning of April 6, 1968. I was in my own bed, in my mother's house, and it was a sunny morning, though no sunshine was shining on me as I looked out of my window, down the driveway, out to Edgewood Street. The apartment building that was less than 25 feet away, cast a shadow on my window, and was the only other view from my vantage point. Ordinarily, being here would have been a treat at this point in the semester. Spring football practice at UConn had been cancelled on Friday. It was the day before my mother's 40th birthday, and that likely would have meant I would get to party with all of my aunts and uncles and cousins and family friends. But there was an emptiness in the pit of my stomach and a gnawing pain in my spirit. I was grieving the assassination of Dr. Martin Luther King, who had been shot down while standing on a balcony in Memphis, just two days before.

My creative writing professor had assigned the class to write something that expressed how we felt about what was going on in our country. The Civil Rights Act of 1968 was on the table as a follow-up of THE Civil Rights Act of 1964, and Dr. King, and all the other heroes who so nobly offered their lives a ransom for a higher cause, were still marching to make it significant. I wanted to do a work that Dr. King would have been proud to hear. As importantly, I wanted to show some of the haughty in my class, that people like me were more than a bunch of 'colored' jocks, but rather young black student-athletes who sought the same opportunities they took for granted.

In my melancholia, I reached for my duffle bag that had my notebook in it and began to write:

'I rise and I look around me; I see fear, anguish, and pain.
The days of my life flee from me, but hopes and dreams remain.'

"What's Going On?" contains responses to social and/or political circumstances that have been driven by "whispers" of inspiration.

We are in a season when the world is changing at an accelerated rate; distances between nations are shrinking due to advances in transportation and communications; cultural differences are diminishing due to exposure to foreign cultures, and thus we are constantly rewriting the standards that our children are to recognize; science and technology are transforming our fantastical excursions into the frontiers of tomorrow into the commonplace of our today; the efficiencies gained in our real life allow one man to do the job of many, and from a place far distant from the place that pays for the end result of that effort; the wealthy are gaining wealth at a rapid pace because of their positioning within the new world economy, and the middle is being pulled out as the jobs go away, and as they tumble to move the poor off of their precarious perches.

We yet have hope! Keep Christ central in your life and He will provide the way; not so much by miracles, but by doing a work in you that will equip you to handle the coming season, and to grab prosperity from the hands of discouragement!

Good Morning World

I rise and I look around me; I see fear, anguish, and pain.

The days of my life flee from me, but hopes and dreams remain.

I rise and I see the darkness, where dim lit dreams are lying.

They scream hopes for peace, but the truth they are denying.

I rise and look inside of me to see if the answer's hiding there,

But answers are concealed from me, in the fortress of my despair.

I rise and see our leaders: charismatic, witty, and sunny.

But they're racist hatred feeders, who care less for us than money

I rise and I see poor families, with no bread upon their tables,

A starving child just one year old; parents trying but still unable.

I rise and search this whole world, and find greed is fueling hate.

War flags overseas unfurled, while homeland battles just must
wait.

I rise and I look behind me, and see that life was once much
worse,

But the Word of God reminds me; unless we change we're cursed.

I rise and I look ahead of me; I see a dark path still unclear.

A dreamer once said to me; great faith keeps great dreams near.

I rise and I look around me; I see a man who foreknew he'd die;

The cost of his courage astounds me; but he willingly paid the
price.

So when I arise tomorrow, may I see promise for great change,

And may we people of great sorrow bring great honor to his name

Let Them Rejoice in Their Dignity

Floating from somewhere in the depths of time,

Rising beyond the beat of hostile drums;

The outraged screams of shackled warriors;

The chilling shrieks of frightened children;

The woeful sobs of anguished mothers;

The scornful laughter of kindred captors;

The tinkling coins exchanging bloody hands;

The indignant words from a cacophony of tongues;

The heavy clanking of a thousand chains;

The endless roaring of the boundless sea;

A prayer is unleashed and delivered on wings of faith, soaring

above the undulating Atlantic.

That faithful soul knew its power and depended on that power to

deliver her people from

The incessant flapping of canvas sails;

The staccato retching of seasick captives;

The sickening splash of jettisoned bodies,

The hollow groan of docking ships;

The inane chatter of curious spectators;

The harsh shrill of callous auctioneers;

The frightening crack of blood drenched whips;

The pulsating clatter of the ravenous cotton gin;

The nervous laughter of confused children;

The pensive wails of child-snatched mothers;

The muffled sobs of ravaged brides;

The silent moans of cuckolded grooms;

The arrogant shout of boys calling men boys;

The deferential whispers of men calling boys "suh";

The resounding report of musket balls:

The sudden bang of the hangman's floor;

Yet still that simple prayer from urgent lips searched a place in

time to deliver the fruit of its promise above;

The jubilant shouts for false liberation;

The exasperated sighs of stark realization;

The intimidating crackle of flaming crosses;

The deafening hush of empty pockets;

The restrictive cawing of old Jim Crow;

The defiant chanting of the freed Negro;

The deceitful patter of Uncle Tom's feet;

The syncopated rhythm of an ingrained beat;

The startling screech of buses stopping;

The primeval roar of dogs snarling;

The angry hiss of hoses whooshing;

The hate filled threats on bullhorns screaming;

The polished rhetoric of politicians lying;

The rib shaking sobs of mothers still crying;

The expectant chorus of 'The Anthem' soothing;

The pounding of fists while Rap's rapping;

The brothers running while Malcolm's dying;

The hate filled rants of Strom fronting;

The sad report of John, Martin, and Bobby falling;

The collective weeping of a nation grieving;

The innocent blood of centuries slowly drying;

The tinkling of glass ceilings cracking;

The hollow thud of opportunity knocking;

The rusty creaking of hinges long unmoving;

The ardent cursing of bound freed men awakening:

The fading echoes of Martin's dream yet soaring;

That urgent prayer that seemed to dance from one frustrated

landing place to another still ascended to elude;

The exciting clang of school bells swaying;

The splashing of black feet in Nam's paddies decaying;

The urgent rustling of E-Z Widers rolling;

The Zippos flipping while the heroin's cooking;

The pimps slapping their brothers' sisters whoring;

The woeful crying of abandoned babies starving;

The silent screaming of their aborted brothers evaporating;

The shaky whining of the crack whore pleading;

The cracking of nines over engines gunning;

The gut wrenching sobs of mothers in mourning;

The "brothas" calling each other dogs laughing;

The same sissies calling their sisters bitches abusing;

The shouting of Gang-stars keeping it real warnings;

Their Benz's purring home to suburbia 'hypocracizing';

The rattling of chains as we stay behind doors hiding;

The newsman counting the lives still wasting;

As if frustrated by time the prayer seemed to be meandering
steadfastly into oblivion but then came a new Rap rapping amidst;
The false prophesying of pundits blasting;
The hope of change sent forth on butter churning;
The money mongers on their own jam slipping;
The stench of their bread in their toaster burning.
The promises of jobs over oceans scoffing;
 The foreclosure signs in front yards clacking;
The song of the Kenyan's son enticing:
The cheers of the world's children hoping;
The pounding hearts of black men casting
The votes gained by their fathers' dying;
The harmony of ballot boxes clicking;
The seeds of hate a time bomb ticking;
The plotting of old boys in panic crying,
The fulfilled millions on one dream relying
Yes, floating from the timeless shores of despair, somehow, an
overcoming prayer soared, seeking a place to land on an unseen
mountaintop of hope; not that God's ear was infertile nor was He
unmoved. He heard her plea before it passed her quivering lips,
and since that time He calls a people to a feast of blessings that
requires nothing but obedience and a loving heart to partake in.
One dream grabbed the wings of that prayer and soared for forty
more years, and then, before two million attending and billions
more watching through eyes unseeing, that prayer from the
motherland for her captured kings and queens and princes and

princesses and priests and teachers and doctors and warriors and mothers and fathers and still suckling babies, lifted nearly 4 centuries ago, fell as a dove of blessing upon the shoulders of the seed of her son.

"Oh wise and merciful God, whatever we are to learn from this exile; whatever we are to gain from all of this grief; let us not forget that we are the sons and daughters of kings; and more so that we are your children. When our searching has found a place of freedom, let our people never again sell each other into slavery; and when the bondage of the scars of our affliction has passed, let our children prosper, and let them never again defile, defame, degrade, denounce, or destroy one another, but rather let them rejoice in their dignity!"

Imus Got Fired

Imus got fired just the other day, for words misspoken.

I mean, he got justly fired the other day for misspeaking words.

It was not as much about what he said but of whom he spoke.

Sullying virtuous icons of black femininity was his first error.

Thinking it was hip to emulate the brotha's was the second.

Our super hip, super slick, super greedy young black brotha's.

Oh you know who they are; imitating intimidating.

Selling poison for a dollar; hustlers of all stenches!

Pimping our mothers and sisters and daughters for trinkets.

Playing our sons and brothers like mindless pawns in their perverted game.

Looking like their fathers who sold our people into slavery 400 years ago.

Oh, you didn't know? Yeah they were young black brotha's too!

Oh you know who they are; 'hypocracizing' hip-hop.

Keepin' it real. Imprisoning minds like a malignant tumor.

Selling a life that feeds sellers of death. Keepin' it real.

You are slowly turning our people into caricatures of fools.

They foolishly look to you as one who can lead them thru. How blind they are.

Can't they see you drive off in your Benz headed for the 'burbs.

There you'll strip the baggies for Armani's and head to the office,

To dissect the demographics to plot more profit for pain.

Remember this; all rich men aren't wealthy nor are all wealthy men rich.

Meanwhile our kids can't calculate; can't conjugate; don't communicate.

Money is king at any price, at anyone's expense.

Hating each other, and going for bad with everybody.

Your songs call us the unspeakable and our women ho's and bitches.

And we are forced to listen to your songs being sung by Imus.

They claim they can't understand why they can't sing your songs on the radio.

Certainly we lift you for saying what we put Imus down for.

You professors of hatred that kill our sons for fabric colors;

Who portray our beautiful queens as booty bouncing sluts;

Stop allowing them to use your words as boomerangs;

They hide behind your music as they turn up the volume.

They play your words to your people and we must listen.

Yeah, Imus got fired just the other day, but was it just...?

Was it just him speaking hate, or him speaking just like you?

Voting for Obama

Today I stood beneath a tree; its broad branches a canopy over a large grassy courtyard.

Six large men, holding hands, arms extended, would barely circle her broad trunk.

I was in Virginia under such a tree, and I could scarcely avoid asking my question of her, silently:

"Were you here? Were you here when my people trudged past your spindly arms, when this commonwealth held no wealth for those who were common to the shores of Africa?

"Did you ever feel the sting of the rope that used your stability to suddenly stop the downward lunge of a dark man accused of nothing more than seeking to be a man?

"Did you ever feel the forced, naked embrace of a mother who simply sought to protect her child; her body shielding you from the blood that the snake drew from her back as he hissed against her time and time again?

"Did you ever serve as the cathedral for the faith filled prayers of frustrated dreamers?

"Did you ever hear them dare to whisper their audacious hope that a day such as today would ever come to pass?"

I dared not speak my inquiry aloud, not so much that there were scores of all races and hues around me, neither was I concerned that such words might arouse either emotions or commotions from those who might be otherwise focused on such a reverential occasion, but more that I dared not speak, so full was my heart.

There, under that tree, a silent ambassador to the past, I was about to do what even I dared not dream. I stood, as did many others in the long line, to vote; to entrust the future of this great nation, dedicated to freedom and equality and bravery, into the hands of the son of a people that were not free, and legally declared unequal, by the cowardly and the unjust who ironically assigned the broad powers to the office he was seeking.

I wondered if they were turning in their graves; or jumping higher in the eternal fires they danced in. Assuredly they weren't smiling down from heaven.

How grateful was I that the rains that threatened kept their promise, and danced between the openings of the dense canopy above. As they fell upon my face, I rejoiced that I now had manly cause to wipe the water that threatened to leap from the mounds of my cheeks. Today I stood beneath a tree and could swear I heard her whisper "Hallelujah!"

Tears of Joy

As if draining a wound, my body released its flows;

Not from an open sore but from a closed space in my heart.

My tears flowed uncontrolled; relieving pressure from a malady.

A malady I did not know I had, nor could I escape.

It was primal; the scream rising from deep within seeking release.

A scream that eluded voice and flowed through my eyes instead.

I could not scream because my voice was otherwise occupied,

With shouts of praise, and adulation, and Hallelujahs!

As I danced in circles on knees too stiff to dance on,

I became aware that a dreamer's dream was this night awakened.

I realized that millions of prayers were that night answered.

I remembered those who dared not even dream to pray for this.

I saw thousands of faces of all hues weeping and rejoicing.

Through tears of joy I mourned Martin; I prayed for Barack.

Be Ever Courageous

We stand in awe of brave men and honor them in our
remembrances;

Their fearless acts, their thoughtful deeds, their selfless
motivation;

Inspires us to emulate them in our times of need; in times like
these;

We pray for fearlessness in giving our all for family, friends, and
nation.

Yet it is fruitless to seek fearlessness for it is ether: a phantom.

I believe no man faces danger fearlessly; though many with
courage.

I consider courage the stuff to envy, for it is the brave man's elixir;

Men dedicated to overcoming their fears, both real and imagined;

Understanding that God has not given them the spirit of fear:

Knowing they have great power through their creator and His
provision;

That true love is bourn from a decision to care more for others
than self;

And that they are blessed with a sound mind that sorts reason
from emotions.

I appreciate your courage, brave sons who jeopardize your lives
for our freedom,

For you live to serve; and overcome the fear of danger by your
resolve and faith.

We should remember you when we are vexed by those fears that so easily beset us;

We should understand that most fears are just false evidence appearing real.

We too should gather our weapons and march resolutely into life's battles.

Putting our trust in God for our next moment, we should be ever courageous.

No Regrets

If I never sail the ocean, for fear of the raging sea;

Nor pull too hard on life's restraints for fear of breaking free;

If I never listen closely afraid of what I'd hear;

Or seek to hide in yesterdays, to subdue tomorrow's fear;

Or if I never seek the truth for fear of what I'd see;

Or let others' thoughts control my own so they'd think well of me;

Then I'll betray myself, and I'll live my life a lie,

For if I live in fear of life, then from birth I began to die.

So I'll live my life and enjoy it, and praise God for the tests that come;

For I'd rather be sorry for the things I've tried, than regret what I've never done.

For dreams are far too precious, and my chances much too few

To let my quest of caution's rest keep dreams from coming true.

A Light Brighter Than Day

When it all seems to fall to pieces, and it seems the good you've done

Is poured out like yesterday's chicken grease as a hazard on your path.

When even the remembrance of the mountaintops you've climbed

Is hidden by the fog lingering in the depths of the valley of your despair

When hope is snatched from your dreams of tomorrows' promise

And all the pages of your plan book beyond yesterday are filled with intrusive nothingness.

When you are forced to stand on dry yet precarious ground at river's edge

As you impotently watch its swift current carry your life's work away

Then you know you are at the crossroad of Givin' Up and Livin' Up!

Where the road from what had been forks into the paths of that which will be!

One smooth and very broad; devoid of curves without many hills to climb

Getting anywhere is not expected because going nowhere is the norm.

Having invested all, it is the easy way for those who mourn a future gone,

Where fatigue steals dreams that are forgotten as they race down its straight ways

And hope hitches a ride as they both disappear over a pitiful horizon

Where nothing ventured soothes the fear of losing that which you cannot gain.

The other is rough with pulse raising horizons that hide behind the mystery of every curve.

It leads over mountains high and valleys low where ease quickly yields to distress

But just as quickly despair gives way to the hope of what lies around the next curve

We are exercised by its inclines and we are nourished by the trials of its valleys

Being well prepared we dare to dream and to hope and to be filled with faith

That even in the darkest night, we are guided by a Light that is brighter than day.

A Very Present Help

I never would have figured out how special those "Whispers" were, until I figured out just how real God is in the everyday aspects of my life. It's safe to say that I don't stand alone in my conclusions, but I will speak from my singular perspective because what He gives me will be different from what He gives you. How He works with or through me will be different from how He interacts with you. His design for my life will be different from His design for yours. He will prosper me in ways that He will not prosper you. He will correct me in ways He will not correct you. He will bless me in ways He may not bless you, but we can stand on this common bridge, that carries us safely over the turbulences of life: He is God Almighty, and He loves and cares for us, and He is ready to step into our lives to whatever degree we ask of Him, and have the faith to believe that He will!

That is why so much of what I write is centered on His place in our lives. He wakes me up to address things so that His message can be delivered. I am here to tell you just how beautiful and wonderful He is, and how we can nurture our relationships through Him and with Him.

I pray you will be blessed as I share what He has given me to proclaim Him and exhort you. I give Him all the praise, the honor, and the glory!

Heroes

How many would have suffered, or even died, but for the acts of those that we call heroes?

Their acts of daring filled with caring, overwhelm their fears for self.

How many times have we stood and cheered these acts, and given honor to our heroes?

We sincerely offer gratitude, avoiding empty platitudes, for those who so freely give of self on our behalf.

They save our children, fight our wars, rescue our endangered, recover our lost, lead our people, heal our sick, win our games; those we call our heroes.

And if in trying they end up dying we lift them higher still, for caring turned to sacrifice claims the brightest badge of all.

So how much more does our Lord deserve that highly honored place, for all the souls our Savior saved with one courageous act of grace?

Yet few amongst us cheer His name and give Him the acclaim, as we would a man who makes the score that wins some mindless game.

He saves our children every day, and each day He wins our wars,

He rescues the endangered and they're safe forevermore,

And He alone has power to recover all those who are lost,

He leads His people, His redeemed, for whom He paid the cost.

He heals the sick by those stripes that birthed in brutal pain

And when that final buzzer sounds, His shout will win the game.

Because of the significance of their acts and their impact on our lives, there is no wonder that we are so awe stricken by our fallen heroes;

Yet how much more should we be in awe of all that Jesus did; He became the sacrifice that we might have life and that more abundantly!

We are right in our gratitude and our thanksgiving for having fallen heroes; but a higher call to thanksgiving for Christ is required; because, having fallen, He rose!

I'm So Glad the Masquerade is Over

Lord, You have blessed me with physical and intellectual gifts. I have been able to power my way through life with my physical prowess and to reveal some awesome insight with my intellect. I grew to depend on them and my ability to use them whenever I found they fit into my plan. I certainly had more than enough to excel, yet never enough to fulfill my potential; never enough to be all You have called me to be.

Today, I saw myself from a different perspective. As I looked within, at the reflection in the mirror of introspection, I caught an ugly glimpse of myself. I saw a worn and faded figure, running the curve into the stretch run of his life. During the twilight hours, I turned back to examine the shadow I cast, and I saw a shadow that was filled with broken dreams and unfulfilled promise.

I suddenly understood the problem. I had accepted Your gifts and used them to the best of my ability, but I had not really asked the Giver to guide me in their use, to the best of His ability. I had depended on me and my gifts, instead of on You and Yours.

Now I am glad the masquerade is over, but not my journey. With this mask removed, I truly see my image. Without the darkened glasses, I can truly see Yours. What a fool I have been to have ignored Your stretched out hand. It's not like You weren't my Father. I will stop running now. I want to savor every footstep, but before I walk on, there is something I must say.

Before I move beyond this place, I choose to stand. Here I look up to You and ask Your forgiveness for all of the wasted moments, and hours, and days, and weeks, and months, and years, and decades. I repent of all the broken promises and abandoned dreams. I repent of the distorted priorities that twisted the road You so graciously laid out before me. I repent of all of the betrayals of You and others who have loved me. I repent of my slothfulness in my stewardship of the assets You have placed in my hand. I repent of all the decision points when I depended on me, or others, more than I depended on You. I repent of all the times my knowledge pushed aside Your wisdom and my fears blocked out my faith. I am a man most despicable, yet I know how deeply You love me.

I stand here reaching my hand to You, and I know that You will take it. Now I ask, as humbly as I can, that as I head down the home stretch, will You guide my feet and hold my hand? My spirit tells me that You smiled before You answered, and I smile as I resume my journey with my hand firmly in Yours.

Where Are the Nine – *Luke 17:17*

Lord forgive me, I humbly beg you, for all those many times,

You could not count me that faithful one, but one of the careless nine.

I can't repay you, I don't know how to, there's nothing you need of me,

I simply came to humbly beg you to accept my apology.

For all those times I failed to thank you for all that you have done,

I can't recall them, I couldn't count them if I named them one by one.

Lord forgive me for not returning like that faithful one.

Accept that now I thank and praise you, like a faithful son.

You are so loving, and so gracious, to forgive me of these things,

And to allow me to come before You, to bow before the King.

And Lord forever I shall thank you for the price you paid in blood,

Yet no matter how much I thank You, it would never be enough.

My prayer, Lord, is that from this day I will return to You,

To lift my voice and thank you, for all the things you do.

And when we look back on my life, when my final race is run

I won't be counted in that crowd of nine, but as the faithful one.

Living in a Basement.

I am living in a basement;

You know, at the bottom of the building.

I didn't always live in such a humble place,

But a strange thing happened on my way to the top.

I prayed that a door would open, and was glad when it did.

It barely opened up a crack, when through that crack I slid.

I prayed for favor for my rent and miraculously received it.

My fortunes changed so suddenly, I scarcely could believe it.

I thought I made my mad money by using my sound mind.

I could not see this subtle trap; my spiritual eyes were blind!

I found a lofty place I liked and I decided to move right in.

I stayed and played until I strayed; I had been seduced by sin!

I envied the elite; their lifestyle so sweet that I sincerely yearned to taste it.

To me their wealth signified that they were truly dignified; I envied wealth and chased it.

I did things I detested; but I never did confess it. I was penthouse bound.

To them I seemed legit, but I was a cold hypocrite; no integrity could be found.

I feared being rejected and danced to be accepted; their rhythm was so controlling.

Subverting who I prayed to, I acted just like they do, but man, I was rolling!

Decaying like a cavity from all the depravity from all that milk and honey.

I was hangin' and bangin' and whorin' and scorin' and rollin' in the money;

I dined on thick steaks and cocktails at eight and the necks of some pretty young things.

There were dudes quite dapper and baggy pant rappers, but I never sought The King.

I only waved at God, barely giving a nod, as I passed the stairway to heaven!

Though abundantly blessed, I denied my success was by the Grace that He had given.

I wouldn't use the stairs; with no time to spare, I took the elevator to the top.

Laughing and joking the doors hardly opened; the elevator barely stopped.

I didn't notice the floor as I rushed through the door and then took a sudden drop.

My heart pounded to a beat like stampeding feet; the wind whistled in my ears.

Through this pit black as night, devoid of the light, I was filled with crushing fear.

Blind and unseeing I screamed for some being to save me as I fell.

I was tumbling quite madly, scarred and bruised badly, I yelled, and I yelled, and I yelled.

Then out of the darkness came a voice; a voice to avoid if given a choice; this voice most dark and grim.

Not quite a bark; almost a hiss; this voice calling from my abyss;
Yes, I was terrified of him.

"Yo bro' you just fell and headed straight to hell, but, my man, I
can assist you.

I'll give you great things; you'll dine with great kings; there'll be
none who can resist you."

Then said that voice most dark and grim, "I've watched you run
away from Him, so I lured you with my charm.

I made you rush through that door, into the car that had no floor,
you fell right into my arms.

In you came! You got caught in my game! Now it's time to settle
the score.

I won't let you drop, but you will need to stop praying to God
anymore."

Then from deep down inside, my spirit man cried, "Resist him
and he will flee."

Like a mourner's moan I heard myself groan, "Satan get away
from me."

"Okay! You can go, but surely you know your landing will be
your end.

You've fallen from grace. He can't stand your face. He won't take
you back again!"

Then I said, "No more conversation! Here's my observation;
you're talking about my Father,

The One who dismissed you and those who assist you, so you
really needn't bother!

I've opened my eyes and I now realize, the error of my ways
But I am content that if I just repent, He'll forgive me this very day!
So I'll repent my fall, but it's really His call, whether I continue falling.
But I assure you of this, I'm equipped to resist, so be gone. You're defeated. Stop stalling."
In a flash he was gone. I was tumbling headlong, as natural forces propelled me.
Then as soon as I prayed, my freefall was stayed as a loving hand upheld me.
"I heard your voice as you made your choice between mammon and My calling.
And now that grace, that your deeds can't erase, has come to ease your falling."
It hurt when I landed, but I understand it was the crash that comes with climbing.
I brushed myself off. I wheezed and I coughed. This darkness was so confining.
Still limping and sore, I sought the first floor, but could not find the stairs.
Had I lost my sight? I could not see the light, and I wondered if any was there.
I wept and I prayed. I was so dismayed that I had fallen so far from the top
I felt lost in this place, and here only by Grace, there is no lower

place to drop.

So I desperately prayed, that a door be displayed, and when it was I moved right in.

And the cost of my rent was the Son God had sent; who paid my price for sin.

So I found a new pace in a more humble place, not so high and lifted up.

Though not an obscenity, it lacked some amenities, but not bitter in my cup.

It took me a while to embrace my lifestyle, the change was so abrupt.

In a room with one view, my choices are few; my only view is up.

I watch haughty fools, or rather their shoes, as they hastily come and go.

They wear sling backs and mules, and brogues fit for fools, all scrambling to and fro.

Like mannequins in pretty clothes, with painted smiles and empty souls, they rush to meet their friends.

Mindless clones they hardly know, meeting in places that they shouldn't go; they rush to meet their ends.

Coming and going without caring or knowing where their old friend had gone.

They seemed unaffected but you had to expect it; they had been so blind for so long.

Sometimes I look up and close my eyes, and see soft clouds floating in sunny skies, and find a sense of peace.

I'm not up there any longer, but inside I'm feeling stronger, and I feel my joy release.

I am back to that place, where resting on Grace, I will never again depart.

My soul seeks my Lord. My faith is restored. Hope lives and I take heart.

I constantly read and I pray; I laugh and I heal each day; I cry because I feel loved.

Darkness and gloom have fled from my room as God's Son alights like a dove.

Yes, now I am living in a basement. You know; at the bottom of the building,

But it is a lofty place, and I will never again live in abasement.

Don't Call God Religion

Consider the wonders of this world and the miracle that is man
Can't you see this life is not by chance but that someone has a plan?
Before your mother gave you birth, Christ knew you by your name.
And He knew the day would come, you'd deny Him to your shame.
He understands all your fears. He came to share your pain.
He knows you're ugly deep inside, and He loves you just the same.
Still He came to give you hope and counted not the cost.
To save you from the price of sin, He suffered on that cross.
So don't call God "Religion" like some thing or tale untrue
In your heart you know He's real, though you often side with fools.
For the fool has said there is no God and speaks boldly in disdain,
But when in need he must concede, He calls upon His name.
"Oh God" he cries, "I'm so afraid. Of this danger that I face."
Then stands amazed when he too is saved by God's amazing Grace.

To Please the Heart of God

If I believe within my heart, that there is nothing I can't do,

And in my heart there is no doubt that the Word of God is true,

Then whatever I can imagine, will be mine to claim,

If I boldly go to God in faith, and ask in Jesus' name.

Yet doubts still attack my mind, and seek to reach my heart

But hope and faith are bonded there and can't be torn apart.

I know Faith comes by hearing, and hearing by His Word,

And that the just shall live by faith, and of this I am assured.

At every crossroad of my life; when I've stopped to look behind,

Life's trials and the Word of God define this faith of mine.

So now I boldly look beyond what eyes of flesh can see,

And look ahead through eyes of faith, at what's ahead for me.

And if doubts arise that I'm equipped to reach that lofty place

I must eliminate the doubt so faith can fill that space,

And know that I am guided by His Word, His staff, and rod,

And if I live my life by faith, it will please the heart of God.

How Can God Be Everywhere?

"How can God be everywhere?" I've heard the skeptics ask.

Even for God, to be everywhere, seems much too great a task.

How can He hear all our prayers and hear us all at the same time?

Do you think that it's impossible? Well, this will blow your mind.

No doubt you surf the internet to get some info that you need,

It provides the required info, and responds at lightning speed.

And it's not only you that seek, but there are millions at one time

They're seeking from all places, these millions of different minds.

And it answers all their questions, and most answers we can trust

How much more can God provide, than men He made from dust?

If God made man He made man's mind, so it comes as no surprise;

Man's mind cannot perform like God's, because God is much more wise.

God's Football Team

There was a young man playing sandlot football.

He was getting knocked around a bit, but The Lord was watching him and the Lord noticed that he had some talent so He went and knocked on the young man's door and said, "How would you like to come and play on my team?"

The young man got excited and said sure Lord I'll come play on your team.

The Lord said "That's good, but there are two rules that I want you to observe. The first one is that you have to believe in all that I tell you to do. The next one is that you have to rely solely on me. Now the field that you're going to be playing on is called Sanctification. One end zone is Hell and Damnation and the other end zone is Glorification."

The young man chose his own team and he had players on his team like A Little Faith, Self-Righteousness, and Love, and Goodness, but he also had some weak spots on his team like a Little Doubt, Old Nature, Knowledge, Pride and Self-Reliance. They were playing against Satan's team, and Satan's team had an awesome line-up. On the line there were Lust, and Greed, and Covetousness, and Lies. And the linebackers were Fear, Doubt, and Guilt; and the corners were Blasphemy and Evil and the safeties were Death and The Grave.

The boy would play a little and gain a little bit of ground and get knocked down. Sometimes Pride would get in his way and He would get sacked by Lies and Greed. And sometimes he would rely on Knowledge to gain him some ground, but he always seemed to fumble the ball. But then there were plays that he would rely on The Lord and He found that his Little Faith went a long way. They kept struggling on down the field, and as the game wore on, the young man got stronger because he became more aware that when he relied on the Lord, his plays met with more success. And on the last play, as time was running out, he went to run across the goal line to Glorification, but Death and The Grave were blocking his path but Amazing Grace raced across the field and delivered a crushing block to both of them and the young man sprinted across the goal line.

Now when he got across the goal line, God, who owned the team, was cheering him on and saying "Well done my good and faithful servant." Then the Coach, who is The Holy Spirit, asked, "Would you like to see the game the way that We saw it?"

The young man, a bit confused, said yes.

God said, "Even though I am the CEO, Jesus is the offensive coordinator, and The Holy Spirit was calling all of the plays. You were actually playing with a spiritually superior ball called Justification." The boy watched as the game film unfolded.

He was deep in his own territory with his back to the enemy's goal line of Hell and Damnation. And Satan's team was bearing down. But as he looked out over his team, he noticed that he had some new, more stalwart looking players replacing those that had not done such a good job in the game he had just played. At the center was His Belief, and the guards were Grace and Love, and

Patience and Joy were his tackles. Prayer replaced Self Reliance on the end, and Righteousness was flanked far to the right and Faith filled the slot where a Little Doubt once stood. Goodness and Mercy were the running backs, and he was the quarterback and the name across his back was New Nature. Belief snapped Justification to his New Nature and Grace pulled to lead the play. Faith blocked out Doubt and Joy overwhelmed Fear. Patience knocked out Guilt, and Prayer overcame Lust, Love took on anyone not blocked because Love can overcome a multitude of sins. Belief runs down field to take on Blasphemy and Righteousness crushes Evil, so as he ran down the sidelines of the valley of the shadow of death, he had no fear of Evil, and he saw that his New Nature was sweeping the end with Grace leading the way, but he noticed that something else was different, because he noticed that his New Nature was running with more power and speed. As he looked closer, it was no longer him running down the field, but it was Christ who lives in him. As he moved down the field, racing towards Glorification, Death and The Grave were Satan's last hope to stop the play. These two terrors were zeroed in on Christ and aimed their assault at Him, but Christ ran right through Death and overcame The Grave. Running behind him as an escort was Goodness and Mercy and they followed Him all the days of his life and He dwells in the House of the Lord Forever.

On Red and 'Pank'
And Shades in Between

The most influential person in our life is our mother. Not to say that fathers don't greatly affect us, because they do, but our mothers are our comfort zone. Any stumbling child will call out one name as soon as they hit the ground; Mommy! It's the way God planned it, for she is the bowl in which we are mixed, the oven in which we are baked, and the platter upon which we are presented. Our life comes through her. Our sustenance comes from her. And our comfort comes in being near her. She is the first person we say that we would die for, and she is the last person we would ever want to hurt. Her voice can soothe us to sleep as well as stop us in our tracks. If we can only afford one gift, it's for her. If there is only one seat in the room, it's for her. If there is only one chocolate left in the box, even under weak protest, it's for her. Her position in our lives, if she is worthy of the name, can't be replaced by anyone else, and we revere her all the days of our life.

I was blessed to live in a house where my mother's mother also lived. They were as different, at that point in their lives, as they were alike. My mother was almost six feet tall; my grandmother was barely five-five. My mother slender; my grandmother had grown a bit stout with age. My mother would take a social drink rarely; my grandmother sipped wine, almost daily. My mother smoked cigarettes; my grand-mother dipped snuff. My mother loved to play Pokeno; my grandmother loved to play the numbers. My mother was great at cooking on top of the stove; my grandmother specialized in baking, (although my mother took over a domain that my grandmother had prepared her to take over). But where they were alike was in their gentle but assertive ways; their sharp minds; their being slow to wrath; their unwillingness to spare the rod; their joy in laughter; their faith in God; their caring for people; their love for family; their encouragement of their children and their grand-children.

I watched as the years turned tomorrows into yesterdays and their roles kind of flipped. As best we can tell, my grand-mother was 100 years old when she died in December of 1985. As she grew weaker, I watched as my mother willed herself stronger so that she could provide my grandmother nurture and care and honor and respect and love until the day she died.

As long as I can remember, my love for them was so strong that I sought to fulfill their highest hopes for who I would become. In watching them, and experiencing them, I learned to love. In honoring them by my life and by my tributes and my commitment to their legacy of love, I feel that the greatest substance of their prayers have been answered. So it is in their honor that I present my writings to them and about them, and to all mothers as well.

The Discipline of Love

If things go as I hope, I will bury my mother, and she not
me.

Not that I fear death and want to outlive her, seeking the
milestones of longevity,
But rather for love, that she not suffer what I think would be
beyond her ability to bear.
Parents aren't meant to bury children, for that is a disruption in
the succession of life.
When her time comes, I'll stand in the sanctuary and glorify my
inheritance: not of riches but of wealth,

A wealth born by the wings of prayer and delighted by the
discipline of love.

For love is a discipline and not an emotion; a decision not a
feeling; a destination not a journey.
She has taught me to love my progeny; to represent God in the
lives of my children.
As faithfully as the moon represents the sun and reflects His light
in the nighttime sky,
So must I reflect the love of God in the lives of those who are my
inheritance from Him.
Many were the nights when the moon was all there was to light
my way,
But always the morning would dawn as dependably as the sun

had set, and the Son would light my world.

When the Son rises I bask there, for He warms and nurtures me; He exposes my path; He unmasks my enemy.

Even when clouds come, and bring the rains and winds that sweep signposts from my path; even then He shines.

When I have tumbled from the path and was tricked to think I could climb mountains of loose shale;

When I've rolled through the briars and am covered in thorns and thistles and I am drenched in mud;

Though my skin is scraped away and my garments are torn and the stench of the dung of dogs covers me;

When I stand in my nakedness and in the foulness of my filth, nose running, eyes pussy, feet foul and blistered;

Even then He shines upon me; even then His love warms me; even then He shows me the way.

For His love, His light, depends not upon my condition but His position; and He decided to hang upon His love.

I pray that I might play the moon to His Son that I might light the nights of my children.

That I might proffer to them the same degree of grace that He has so freely proffered to me.

That I might truly practice the discipline of love and not be vexed by the fires of my emotions.

That my children might look at me and know the one they see and know my love will not change.

That they might look at me and see that I love them not for what they do, but simply because of who they are.

That they look at me and see that I represent Him, and great is the honor of the representative of a worthy master.

If things go as I hope, my children will bury me, and me not them. For so deep is my love that I feel I could not bear to suffer my life without them.

It would be better that way, for such is the design of the succession of life.

And when they stand before the sanctuary, may they lean on the strength of the One who shines within,

And glorify the Lord for giving them a moon that reflected the Light in their dark and lonely nights

And that they were left with wealth born on the wings of a thousand prayers and delighted by the discipline of love.

I Mimic You

In many ways I mimic you, to my children's benefit.

I never realized how wise your counsel until I became a counselor in search of wisdom.

I now understand your encouragements were your highest hopes in my greatest dreams.

Your discipline was a guardrail on the rocky road of life until I learned to navigate the curves.

How high your joy at my successes, like a balloon I could grab to take me beyond my own elation.

How strong the parachute that caught me in my freefalls, having danced too close to the edge.

How deep your pain when you could not protect me from the chastisement of The Father.

Though even in my times of trouble your presence strengthened me; so I too became a balm.

When I hurt, nothing soothed like the touch of your hand; so now I rub my children's brow.

I never knew the depths of your love; until the Lord taught me too, to love deeply.

Nor did I know the depths of sacrifice in your giving until through love I gave sacrificially.

You poured wisdom, encouragement, discipline, joy and, most of all, love into this empty vessel,

And you rejoice as I overflow into the cups that rest around my table.

The Influence of Your Love

Long after the rays of the sun have kissed,

the last of our earthly days;

And those who are but children now,

have long since gone their way;

As long as the sun shines bright above,

and lights the bright skies blue,

Those generations yet to come,

will all be touched by you.

Those names that are yet unspoken;

whose days are yet unseen;

Whose minds can't yet imagine

the dreams they'll dare to dream;

Your progeny who are yet unborn;

yet a spirit with God above;

When they come they will be embraced,

by the influence of your love.

A Song for My Mother

You might think it goes unnoticed. It may seem that I don't care
But I've seen your every sacrifice. I know you're always there.
Mom I just want to thank you, for all you've done for me
When I was blind you took the time and your wisdom helped me
see
The errors of my ways; when I was living life unsaved,
I was throwing life away, oh Mom, but you never gave up on me

You endured the pains of birth for me, you set aside youth's
worth for me
You fed my body and mind for me, you always found the time for
me,
When I was sick you cared for me, your wealth was never spared
from me,
When I fell you always reached for me, your faith stood in the
breech for me,
You faithfully believed in me, though at times you were deceived
by me,
You labored night and day for me, you hoped, you dreamed, you
prayed for me,
You feared, you laughed, you cried for me, your dreams fell and
they died for me
It's love at the epitome, the Godly way you've mothered me.

Well it hasn't gone unnoticed. Your wise words were not unheard.

And when I was making choices, I remembered every word.

Mom I just want to thank you, for all you've done for me

When I was blind you took the time and your wisdom helped me see

The errors of my ways; when I was living life unsaved,

I was throwing life away, oh Mom, but you never gave up on me

That Christ like attitude in you, brings forth my gratitude for you.

I cherish every smile from you, I'd run a thousand miles for you,

I stand up to life's tests for you, I strive to give my best for you,

My loyalties belong to you, my heart is full of song for you,

I never could return to you, the loving ways I learned from you.

I bend my knees and pray for you, I thank the Lord each day for you

So many times you've prayed me through, my life has been so blessed by you.

Mere words cannot convey to you, what words alone can't say to you,

I know my words aren't strong enough, and no song could be long enough to speak my love for you,

But I hope these few words will suffice to thank you for your sacrifice, and all you've helped me through.

Well it never went unnoticed, and I said in every way I could

That yours are the wings that lift me; the rock on which I stood.

Mom I just want to thank you, for all you've done for me

When I was blind you took the time and your wisdom helped me

see

The errors of my ways; when I was living life unsaved,

I was throwing life away, oh Mom, but you never gave up on me

The Essence of Pink

A tribute to Theresa "Pinky" Fauntroy Cohen

Long, silver, silky, thinning braids bathed in Apex Glossatina fell on the shoulders of her pale green flowered housedress. Braids spun by hands well-muscled and too large for a woman; still weaving though gnarled by the signature of "autheritis", so symptomatic of the toils of life as a 'colored' woman of her time. She gets the best chair and sits there as if hugged in the arms of a loving friend; her chair, and hers alone, and none would sacrilege or risk harm to sit there. From there she commands attention without ever demanding any, for she is well loved.

Her morning coffee was bathed in Carnation milk and thickened with Jack Frost. She gleaned the Courant to see what happened in the world last night: to see if any names she recognized floated by her gaze in the obituaries. If she had a dream, she studied the Dream Book to see if the corresponding number made sense, but more often than not she would labor a good portion of her morning researching and ciphering the records she so diligently kept on sheets yellowed by time and thinned by years of hope filled use. Her forehead was broad and furrowed and well defined, a trait I share, as do many. Under that strong brow were soft gray eyes, though clouded by time, still smiling, for she is well loved.

By her right side, in the shadows of her chair, hid her cup, a tin can laid bare; a partner to the little tin of Buttercup on the table, with her ciphering and glasses. Her tweezers and a mirror lay near her white Bible with the page marker of silk, weighted with the gold-capped crystal ball that held the tiny golden mustard seed. Just behind the chair, well within reach, was Taylor Sherry capped with a plastic cup; a yellow cup with metallic sparkles, faded and stained, having survived the Bon-Core years. You knew not to interfere with "The Price is Right" or mess with any of her stories. She would watch the late movies until the stations went off, then quietly make her way to bed, in peace, for she is well loved.

On her left side the cane leaned against the wall; a sure support and a quick weapon. In the times before the cane, she showed us how to do the "Pickin' Cotton" and "Ballin' the Jack". In later years the cane gave way to the horse and spared the younger generations. She would stand with great effort, her knees having suffered more than her hands. As she walked, you could see the strength in her calves, which were noticeably bowed. It was not unusual for a dozen or so of her grandchildren and their friends to gather at her feet,
listening to tales and watching Tarzan movies, and 'monister' movies on Saturday afternoons. Nor was it unusual for any of us to delight in being able to do her bidding, for she is well loved.

Butter rolls were her signature culinary creation, but not her singular culinary achievement. The holiday season was a time to wonder at the intricacies of her Hog's Head Cheese. She could skin an eel or catfish with the best of them, and prepare them as a delicacy. Her grandchildren loved to scour the woods and briars of Edgewood Street and Flatbush Avenue to uncover the delicious wild blackberries that we would pick and lay before her almost as homage; in part to apologize for berries that never made it home; in part to beg for her fresh berry pies. And though, at times, we were "Minnie Jackameenas" and "Pop Eyed Snakes", we were proud to bring before her our friends, and mates, and children to share her precious love and wisdom, for she is well loved.

I remember my first day of school when my grandmother walked me a mile on seventy-year old legs, framed by aching joints; and those heavy black two-inch heeled shoes. She wore a kerchief in the traditional manner, and she had on a housedress, and a pink cardigan. As she left the classroom, smiling and waving, it was the first time I recall being called by my God-given name; Thomas. As I watched her leave, she seemed so old to my young eyes, and I wondered how much longer....? But I got to watch all she became over the next thirty years, and I was blessed to bring 'Pank' my best friends, my special girls, my bride and both my children; and I got to kiss her moments after... I no longer weep for her, for I still feel her essence in my being, and I love to honor her memory, for she is well loved.

In the Fullness of His Time

A pink rose bloomed on a red rose vine; a natural oddity

And there through sunshine and through rain, she blossomed
faithfully.

From a small pink bud to a beautiful rose, she grew on that old
rose vine.

For years God blessed, for years she bloomed, and withstood the
tests of time.

The Lord would come and gather some, and some would fade
and fall.

Her petals faded, and some petals fell, yet she survived it all.

Then one day our Lord came to take His Pink rose home,

And one of His hosts asked Him why this one had stayed so long.

The Lord then said "My dear sweet child, though she was faded,
scorched, and dry,

I let her stay so very long for it was pleasing to My eyes,

And though in your eyes it may seem this one had stayed too
long,

I used each petal as it fell to make her children strong.

I held her close and loved her much and made all her burdens
Mine,

And I brought her home to live with Me, in the fullness
of My time.

If I Could Taste Just One More Bite

The joyous promise of the next moment

Is wasted on those who fail to cherish its uniqueness

And thus it seduces us with complacency.

At some point, time stops running out so slowly.

Like sand through a tight clenched hand

That grows more fatigued by the moment.

If I could but taste just one more bite

Of those pies and cakes and rolls,

But those not yet baked will never be,

And the recipe is gone.

I am so glad I got to eat my fill.

I remember she smiled as I enjoyed it.

With a grateful smile I said "Thank You"

With a proud smile she said "Glad you enjoyed it"

Now I can smile because I did.

The Persevering Mother

The one who prays while others sleep
That the Lord would find a way to keep
Her children from the tests of life
Or help them rise above the strife.
On many nights she goes to bed
Hungry but her kids get fed;
The one who walks 4 miles each way,
At the start and close of every day.
She tries to make her home a place
Of peace and love and full of grace.
She smiles a lot and fights back tears.
This test has lasted many years.
The one who finds it hard to rest
With work undone, she gives her best,
And prays some more to God at length
To guide her path; to give her strength;
To do her job; to heed her call;
To lead her children through it all.
The one whose kids when they are grown,
Will never leave her there alone.
They'll not forget what she has done.
She'll bring them through it; every one.
They love her much, and much each other.
God bless the persevering mother.

The Apple Lady

For as long as I can remember, she'd be there every day,
Always bringing apples, she would smile and watch us play.
Later my children, then their children rejoiced to see her too,
She smiled and gave them apples, as she was wont to do.
I recall that in her younger years, her cart was always filled,
Then today it dawned on me, and it made my heart stand still,
She no longer pushed the apple cart, along the rugged miles.
She rarely has apples to give away, but still never fails to smile.
Her life had changed; I missed the signs. It never dawned on me,
That beyond the smiles and apples, was a book I did not read.
So I opened up the pages, and in the latter pages found
That silently she cried for help, but I never heard the sound.
For each time she bought her apples, she paid a dearer price,
But to share the joy she brought, she had made the sacrifice.
I never asked the price she paid for what she so freely gave,
Yet she smiled and gave away, the fruit she should have saved.
So the Lord put on my heart, to provide what she had earned.
So I smiled and brought her apples, and she smiled in return.
Her smile had never failed her, as she watched the children play
But now there's joy behind that smile, as she gives her fruit away.
She reaches out with withered hand and offers me a smile
Along with a big red apple "here this is yours my child."
She smiles again and walks away, as joyful as she pleases,
I make a vow to guard that smile, in the mighty name of Jesus.

For Jesus says if we would give in love to those in need,

He would shower us with blessings and prosper us indeed.

On Fathers and Sons

The two familial titles mentioned most in the Bible are fathers and sons. They are mentioned more, by far, than any other position within the family (wife, husband, mother, daughter, children, brother, or sister). This is not to imply that God sees, or man should consider, any of these other relationships as less precious, but the Father/Son relationship is very important in understanding God's relationship with Christ, His relationship with mankind, and men's relationships with the world.

The son is constantly positioned as an extension of the father, and the father that gives his son Godly direction, usually produces a son who eventually follows his example. The Bible says "Train up a child in the way he must go, *and when he is old* he will not depart from it." The father has historically been called into account for his family's wellbeing, spiritually and otherwise, so a good father that teaches a son well is apt to see a duplication of his household when he visits his son's. The same teaching reaches the daughter, but her position as a wife and mother was not designed to be the one whose headship influences the family to the same extent that a fully functioning husband and father does. Unfortunately, we must acknowledge that our current condition, with so many single parent homes, has forced women to fill that fatherly role, or the children tend to suffer because she is ill-equipped to take the position she has not been trained to fill. Just as much of a problem is a dysfunctional or absent father. Such a man, displayed before his children, can cause a devastating effect on his family that can often take generations to overcome.

It is in the Father Son relationship that our investment in our children most directly assures a perpetuation of our likeness and our name to future generations. I love my daughter in a very special way, and I love my son in a special way as well; but I love them differently. I helped mold her. I shaped him. I protected her. I taught him to be a protector. I helped teach her to be a woman like the best I saw in her mother, and her grandmothers, great aunts, aunts, and cousins. I took charge of teaching him to be a better man than me.

It was not until my daughter, Tamika, was born, and I took on the mantle of fatherhood, that I fully understood the degree of love and protection that comes from our Heavenly Father. It was not until my son, Trevor, was born that I understood the need to be used of God to help shape a life to become my replacement in the cycle of life. I prayed he would become all the best of what I had ever hoped to be. From the physical, to the emotional, the intellectual, and the spiritual, I valued the opportunity to make a better "me".

I have tried to represent The Father in the lives of my children, and it has been in my relationship with my children that I have come to fully appreciate how He deals with me. I have learned how He loves, because that is how I love my children; unconditionally. There may be rifts in the fellowship, but the love and the relationship never change. They might tick me off and lose my favor, but I have never felt merciless toward them. Their actions might not have deserved it, but my graciousness towards them has never been quenched. Even in the midst of all that love, I have never been reluctant to say "No" to their desires when my fatherly wisdom tells me that "Yes" will cause them harm. I want all the best for them: the best of health, great success, comfort in wealth, and an overflowing of joy and happiness, but I can only provide that which I am able to. My Father deals with me in the same way, but He is limitless in His ability to provide, so when I try to imagine how much love drove the Father to send His only Son to save me, I think on the love I have for my children and try to magnify it beyond measure and understand that I still fall short of comprehending the love of God towards us.

Still the father/son relationship is more like the God/mankind relationship than any other. It is the only relationship where one of the primary objectives is to replicate the original. Mankind was made in the image of God. Sons are expected to closely resemble their fathers, and when that happens, there is great joy or, in some cases, lamentation. A good father/son relationship involves almost constant mentoring, with the objective of maximizing the son's position in this world as a man.

It is amazing how closely my relationship with my son parallels my maturation process in the Lord. I want to share some of the communication we have had over the years and you'll understand. Trevor was a division one caliber basketball player, so a lot of our communication was flavored by that experience. I will share the period beginning at his high school graduation to his becoming a father. I am also sharing some of my poetry written for my grand-sons. I pray that some young mother raising a son on her own might be able to teach her son through this. I pray that some young father without a good model might gain some insight on becoming a better father through this. I pray that some boy or some young man might get a better insight into manhood through this. I pray that these words encourage hearts and change lives, in the name of Jesus.

I Hope You Run the Bases Well

To My Grandson Christian Otis at 7

I hope you always get a hit when you come up to bat

And when it's time to play the field may you play well at that.

I hope you always play to win, but most of all play fair

And learn if you expect to win, you must faithfully prepare.

I hope that in your life you find, as well as in your games,

That in defeat or victory, you play the game the same.

I hope that every time you play, you always give your best;

And every time a challenge comes, you'll always pass the test.

I hope you heed your coaches well and take their good advice,

And trust in those who earn your trust, but keep your faith in Christ!

Of all the things I wish for you, that wish is number one

I Hope you run life's bases well, and hit a few home runs.

To Christian at Ten

The best things don't come easily, good success is not appointed.
The man who dreams but will not strive, will wind up
disappointed.
If you really want to be the best, then reach deeper than others do.
Your greatest dreams won't come to life without great work from
you.
Always speak when you are so inclined, but listen when wisdom
speaks,
For in wisdom you'll find all you need to expose the truths you
seek.
Treat every man with due respect, but carefully choose your
friends,
And when you've found a worthy friend, stand with them to the
end.
Don't ever scoff at those who lack, for you do not know their
plight,
But encourage them to reach for more, and to always seek God's
light.
And here's one thing to keep in mind, on your way to being great,
Never serve to someone else what you don't want on your own
plate.
Set your sites on your greatest dreams, then pray and work your
plan,
And do all you do to honor God, and you'll be one great man.

Your Father is a King

My prayer is that your dreams come true

That your hopes are all fulfilled

That you can walk in confidence

That you stand within God's will.

And in that special place you stand

Be aware of this one thing

Like your Dad you're a mortal man,

But your Father is a king!

Crossroads

There are certain points in life when decisions must be made;

Decide where to go from there; weigh the price that must be paid.

The choices are all yours, my son, on which way you will go,

But before your decision there's something you should know.

When you're at life's crossroads, you must look left and right,

But then proceed straight ahead, and keep your goals in sight.

Walk with joy. Keep the faith. And here's my best advice;

You'll make the right decision, if you keep your faith in Christ

No Limits

Some people feel there are limits to what they can become,

But for you at this young age, I can't think of one.

Whatever your heart can dream, that's what you can be,

But you must learn the difference, between dreams and fantasy.

A fantasy is but a thought of what you'd like to be,

But your dreams are the plans you make, and nurture carefully.

A fantasy has no real plan; there's not much that you can do,

But your dreams you can work at, to insure that they come true.

May you dream the boldest dreams, and work to pay their price,

And remember as you seek your dreams, you can do all things

through Christ!

Take Your Shots

Hold on a minute player, I've got a word for you!

I heard that just the other day you knocked down thirty-two.

I bet you liked the feeling; when things all fell just right!

And I bet you wondered why you can't do that every night.

It's all in the resistance that will surely come your way,

And depends on how you adjust, 'cause it changes every day.

You will learn to handle it; because practice gives us might.

It's really not that hard to score, just keep your goal in sight.

So when in life, or basketball, it seems hard to make the plays,

It could be the opposition is playing better on that day,

That's when you must dig deep, and concentrate on this;

There's a chance for you to score, after every shot you miss.

Just shoot each time you get the chance, surely some will go.

And know the plays not over, 'til the final whistle blows.

And when the game is over, and the nets hang still and cold,

I hope you never tired of trying, and kept sight of your goals.

As life goes on, take your shots, and please remember this;

With practice and great effort, it's less likely that you'll miss.

God and Basketball

My team was down, but coming back, there was magic in the air

I jumped, I clapped, I shouted out loud, when I became aware

Of just how excited I had become, by watching men play ball.

I showed more passion for this game, than for the greatest game of all.

It started back in Eden, when we were innocent and free,

Until, lured by the other team, we ate fruit from that cursed tree.

The ball was tossed, the tip was lost, Satan scored a three point goal;

He shamed our face, we lost our place, and he thought he stole our soul,

Our defense, based on innocence, was quickly put to shame,

So the coach allowed our conscience to try and change the game,

That too failed. The team was benched by a mighty cleansing flood,

So the team was given government to pull us from the mud.

But that too failed on Shinar's plain, when Nimrod built his tower,

The team dispersed but what was worse, we were confused and without power.

Then the coach sent faithful Abraham, to lead us to the promise,

But the players broke too many rules, and the refs called fouls upon us.

Our team was falling far behind, so the coach spelled out the rules,

And said we'd win if we followed them, but we still behaved as fools.

The coach was greatly angered, because the law did not suffice,

So he sent in our one last hope, His son named Jesus Christ.

The enemy knew of Him, and tried to lure His allegiance away,

But Jesus dribbled right past that trap, and turned and made a play.

There were still players on His team, who were trying to play by law,

But Christ confounded all their schemes to continue like before.

They were jealous and embarrassed that His moves put theirs to shame,

So they lied and plotted and schemed, but still He controlled the game.

He outmaneuvered Satan, and his evil teammates' lies,

They became so frustrated, that they had Him crucified.

His opponents were rejoicing; The Sanhedrin, and Satan too

When they saw Him carried off the court, they thought that He was through,

But the coach called a timeout, and the announcer dimmed the lights,

And said "Folks you won't believe what just happened here

tonight.

It seems that God's Son, Jesus, is back ready to compete,

I saw Him in the locker room with nail-scarred hands and feet.

He was so badly wounded, I could have sworn that He had died,

But He stands now dressed for battle, with new teammates by His side.

They now called Him Love, and He is flanked by Power and by Might,

With His guards, Grace and Mercy: They are such an awesome sight.

Satan had strong teammates too, Cunning, Lies, Fear, and Deceit.

The opposing team fought feverishly to avoid their certain defeat,

But the lead that they had run up, was quickly wearing thin,

Love scored in bundles and stopped a multitude of Sins.

Just before the final buzzer, Christ went racing down the floor

And slammed the dunk heard round the world, and made the winning score."

Now when I cheer my favorite team, for its heroic sacrifice,

I know that I should so much more, exalt the name of Christ.

When I compare the differences of saving me from loss

There is no greater victory, than that won upon the cross.

So the next time you're surrounded, by a stiff and quiet crowd,

Give Jesus all the glory, be free, be brave; shout loud.

If five young men, deserve our glee just because they scored

How much more should we, with joy, shout and praise the Lord.

A Message to My Son at 21

Sometimes when we are in the storms of life, it is very hard to consider that behind all those clouds and that howling wind is the calm of a peaceful sunrise in a safe harbor; but first we must endure the storms. While we are in the storms it is futile to fight them, but wise to learn how to survive them, come through them, and emerge stronger and wiser and better for the experience. Putting our trust in God, His word has promised that all things will work to the benefit of those that love Him, whom He has called to His purpose.

I could not be more proud, nor the circumstances more appropriate than now, at the shore line of your adolescence, looking into the vast ocean of potential that will define your transition to manhood, to say that you have just passed a tremendous test, with honor and dignity and excellence.

When all men doubted you, even me, and felt that you needed to take time to regroup, you declared to us all that we just didn't know the man that you are destined to be; the man that you have become. Welcome to the club. Take a seat of honor. Welcome to the first semester of Manhood 101

A Song for My Son at 21

They say that you have my eyes. You're tall and big boned too!

That you're cerebral like I am, and your moods swing like mine do,

They say that you possess my ways, that you're faith filled just like me,

That you love to laugh, and live to love, especially family.

And you used sports, just like me, to pay your way through school,

And just like me you are creative, sensitive, and cool.

You love the people that I love, and God knows they love you,

But I pray that we are different in one thing that we do!

I pray that when you're older and wiser, just like me

That the reflection in your mirror is the man you hope to be.

Set your sight upon your dreams and never let them fade

And never let them rest as dreams from efforts never made.

Let no man's words convince you of the things you cannot do,

Because you can do all things through Christ, who loves and strengthens you.

And when like me your days grow short, as you face the setting sun,

I pray your life inspires souls blessed by the good you've done.

The Abyss
Written by Trevor Goode

There's this place I try to get out of;

Constantly, on a daily basis.

I scratch and crawl to see the light

Like a dream where everybody's calling for me...

Like a dream where I'm screamin' for everybody else

But they can't hear me

And at times all I hear are murmurings of loved ones crying for
me

And that hurts...

I am in an abyss that I can't get out of.

There's this place that I'm stuck in

Constantly, on a nightly basis

A pit of darkness and failure that...

That I wear sunglasses in, to disguise the fact...

The fact that I am already in total darkness

Here is where I drown in my own tears

In this darkness overflowing with the tears

The tears of those who love me but I try to ignore those are there

I imagine that all I drown in is my own rivers of mourning

I am in an abyss, that I want to get out of

There's this place that I hide in

Constantly, on a moment to moment basis

Because I can't stand to hear the voices or look in the faces

Of those who have sacrificed their lives

Their lives for someone who is not worthy of their sacrifice

What is there possibly to say to those I have failed?

What is there possibly to say to self?

I have failed me, and confine myself with unbearable punishment

Not freeing myself because I have been in darkness so long

I'm scared what the light might bring

I know they hurt because of me, yet I can't confront myself with

their pain

I am in an abyss that I beg to get out of

There's a place that is holding me back from being

That's it, just being, I want to be

Not anything in particular, just to be again

In half light and darkness 'til I get used to the glaring brightness

Where I can hold up my chin without crying

Do you know why I cry?

Do you know why I punish myself like this?

Because, I can't stand to hear the pain in the voices of those who…

Who sacrifice, who sweat and bleed for me,

Me of all people, the one who has yet to succeed the way…

The way I was supposed to.

MY Dad who has embraced me when he should have…

Should have closed the gate on this abyss

That hurts, to know a man that loves me as closely to…

As closely to God as possible, is left in a hole that he might not...

Might not be able to get out of, because of me

How am I still breathing surrounded by this ocean of tears
eternal...

Eternal in every direction to the point where I see nothingness

Just hear the moans and whimpers of those on shore

I am in an abyss, I need God to get me out of

There is a place, where I suffer yet breathe

It is a miracle that I am here; still able to hear them

I cannot give up on life, though it may seem the easiest thing to do

Because, I still hear moans. They have not given up on me.

God doesn't take me away, yet doesn't rescue me just yet

He lets me suffer long enough to make me understand...

Understand who is in control of me in this darkness

He lets me breathe when others would have drowned 100 fold

I must have a purpose here, don't you think?

God must love me. They must love me too (my phone keeps
ringing).

I am swimming now in the direction where I hear their cries.

I am in an abyss, I am trying to get out of

There is a place, where I have been before

Never this deep though, eyes never confined to nothingness wide-
open

I swim anyway, because there is someone calling for me.

I am so far away, I don't know if I'm swimming to God or to them…

But I keep going on, with no rest behind me or in front of me

Not 'til I can emerge ashore where someone waits for me.

But who waits for me there, which direction am I swimming?

I hear them closer than I now hear God, though I know He's right here.

Father, Mother, Sister are waiting for me and I start to see light.

I start to hear footsteps along this abyss floor to meet me halfway.

I swim harder now when I'm weaker and listen better…

Better when I am blinded by the combination of darkness and tears

I am coming to those who have kept me going.

They talked to me in the darkness. My phone never stopped ringing.

They talked to me in this abyss, they never stopped loving me.

They never gave up on me, not knowing if I would ever pick up again

So I keep swimming on my last breath God gave me

And I will hold them again, and smile again, and laugh again

I am in an abyss, I am swimming out of

Thank you for meeting me halfway. My family was my last breath.

Thank you Jesus! I be! I be again!

A Father's Love

When you fall and all seems lost,

I offer you my hand

Whatever pain your fall has caused,

your best will rise again.

You need a friend, now more than ever.

I stand right by your side.

Whatever you face, we'll face together.

There is no need to hide.

Why should you hide when you're forgiven?

You've already been exposed!

I've seen your wounds; I've seen your shame;

Your tear stained eyes and bloodied nose.

I've heard your cursing and your mourning

I sense your pain and I've known your fear

And when trials attack without warning,

I'll always be right here.

For God has taught me how to love you

Thru His love and grace I see;

On every point I would condemn you

He has forgiven me!

I'm more than your father. I'm more than your friend

Because you are my gift from God.

Potholes

As I was traveling down life's roads, things were running pretty
smooth;
All was well within my life; I thought I'd found my groove.
When suddenly I feel a jolt that shakes my very soul
My vehicle shakes. I hit my brakes. I hit a huge pothole.

As I assess the damages, shock gives way to fear.
The road seems so much darker now, and no help seems near.
"I have no way to fix this mess; I have only worn out tools,
How did I miss the danger signs? I've been such a fool!"

Now what once was confidence has given way to doubt,
"I've assessed the situation; it seems there's no way out.
How could I have come this far and moved so well by plan,
To end up here all broken down? How can I start again?"

Suddenly my mind recalled this light I heard about,
They said I'd find one deep inside; if I just sought it out.
Without much thought I found myself dropping to my knees,
"Lord I've never really called on you, but now I'm asking please

"Lord, it seems I'm stuck in danger here in this place so dark and
cold,
Everything was going smooth 'til I hit that huge pothole!
I know that you could help me make it through this night.

I have no help; my only hope is to hold onto Your light."

Suddenly there was a light, but not one I could see
Yet I knew that it was there, shining deep inside of me.
I can't begin to tell you of the joy that filled my soul
When I turned my face to Jesus, and gave Him the control.

Without a word He spoke of peace, this light within my soul,
Of how forever He's been there, and will never let me go.
He said I should remember that His word is ever true,
And when I call upon His name there's nothing I can't do.

So I began to build again, with broken worn out tools,
And found the more I sought the light, the more that I could do.
I used a lot of elbow grease, and scraped my hands a bit,
But I held on firmly to His light, and vowed to never quit.

In morning's light I looked upon, what seemed so hard to do,
I stood in awe; the truth sank in; by grace I made it through.
They were the darkest hours, in that cold and lonely time,
But every time I turned that wrench, His hand was guiding mine.

"I let you hit that pothole son to slow you down a bit,
So you could learn to trust in Me, and learn to never quit.
Now you can share with others what happened on this night;
How in your darkest hour you held onto the light.

Bleeding hands are merely signs of what I brought you through,

But the blood you see is mostly mine; I gave my all for you!

There will be other potholes in the middle of the night

But now you know to call My name, and hold on to My light!"

To Trev at 24

Oh how fast has ticked the clock that has brought you through these years. Each second seeking its own fulfillment but pushed aside by the more pressing need of those coming behind them.

Look back at all the love and laughter and joy and smiles and sorrow and tears and dread. They each have carried the seconds away with them, and from your perch at the point of now you see them as recollections of things that will never again be as they were.

Understand the fleeting nature of life. 24 years ago I dreamed of what you are now, yet now I can barely recall all that you were then.

Fill your heart full with hope and walk boldly into the rest of your life. Enjoy the 24 hours of every day and cherish the moments and savor the seconds, but mourn them not as they pass....for each moment is sufficient unto itself to bring you the joy of The Lord.

Trophies for His Son

Those bronze and plastic trophies that lined the mantle shelf
Were such impressive emblems; such monuments to self.
Now youth's games are set aside. There's manly work to do;
To let your children see God's face, when they look up to you.
As He trusts you with His treasures, more so He demands;
As you bend to lift your children, stand up and be a man.
A father earns a special prize. His mantle shelf is lined,
Not with statues made of brass, but trophies more Devine.

Milestones

A son is the reflection of his father's highest hopes; a measure of
his fondest dreams.
He is a father's reminder of unrealized potential; the promise of
his second chance.
A son is a student of his father's ways; yet a creator of his own
perspectives.
He is his dad's biggest fan and his father's favorite hero for whom
he fervently cheers.
A father celebrates the milestones of his son; they are among the
highpoints of his life.

A Letter from My Son

Dear Dad,

I am so proud to be called your son. You are a great man in the truest sense of the word. It would be futile to try to put all you mean to me in words. I owe everything I am as a man and as a father to your being a man who followed God in my presence, and taught me of His essence by the power of your presence. Your unconditional love, your priceless wisdom, and your emphasis on God and family; all of these things make you my hero. There is no one I seek more to be like; no one else I would rather call my Dad; no one else I would want to call my best friend.

A Fathers' Prayer

May your children's laughter resound in your halls;

May you be able to lift them every time that they fall;

When they come to your table may they always find bread;

May they never fear evil when they go off to bed!

May they always find wisdom in all that you say

May you grow in that wisdom each time that you pray,

And be ever mindful; you don't father alone,

For yours are God's children and He cares for His own.

Daddies and Baby Girls

In my introductory chapter on "Fathers and Sons", I found an abundance of teaching works that I had written over the past 29 years to guide my son and grandsons into manhood and fatherhood. I found the flavor of the poetry and letters I have written to my daughter is very different. With Tamika, I didn't teach as much as I encouraged; I didn't guide as much as guard, for such is the nature of the relationship between a father and his daughter. Most of what I wrote to her was too personal to include in this collection. Not in the sense that no one else should read it, but it was specifically applicable to her and had less of a universal appeal.

I was no less attentive to her. In fact, she had me all to herself for five years, and I spent the years after her brother was born assuring her that she had not been displaced in any way by her new brother! I was there when she was born, and it was me who was graced with her first smile. I was there to build castles in the sand, go for long bike rides, teach her to draw, sing her lullabies, teach her to play basketball, attend her basketball and tee-ball and soccer games, take her to choir practice, let her sit though mine, attend her parent teacher nights, help her with her homework, drive her to and from her early teen socials, intimidate her dates when she started dating, taught her to drive, took her to all of her pageant rehearsals, cheered her through her pageants, attended her graduation, walked her down the aisle, attended the birth of both of her sons, and helped her in every way I could as she progressed through life.

I always let her know that she was the more "fragile" vessel and the calling of her father and the men in her life was to protect her and to provide for her. Not that she lacked strength, but that God has made the female more delicate and more intricate because she is the vessel through whom He would send His precious children. Without ever using the words, I sent her this message by the very nature of our relationship. "In the physical realm, I'm your rock. Find a rock like me, but always remember, I will always be your rock." The message to my son would have been; "I'll be your rock until you learn to be a rock and then we'll be rocks for each other."

The relationship between a father and a daughter is precious. The value of that relationship often forms a template for her self esteem. It also gives her a measuring stick to determine what a good man should look like. His relationship with his daughter will often determine what she values or disdains in men. It also prepares her to fill in the gaps in helping her mate raise their children.

Men will die for their sons, but they will kill for their daughters! With that being said, it is a relationship built on a very special deep seated love. She will always be his princess, and he will always be her hero.

I pray that these writings will encourage some young woman who lacked a positive "Daddy" image in her home that there is a very special place for her in the heart of God and that He sent a man to demonstrate His love to her. It is unfortunate if that man, for what-ever the reason, was unable to fulfill the role; but God loves her nonetheless. I pray that she absorbs all that I write here and claims it as her own. I pray that this teaches some young man how precious the "more fragile vessel" is in the eyes of God, and how well he should treat her; whether it is his wife or his daughter. I pray that it encourages some father that the love and nurture he provides his daughter will far exceed the value of any gifts he might regret he is unable to provide.

A Pledge Revisited

On the day you were born you opened your beautiful eyes and you smiled at me, and stole my heart.

I vowed so many things at that moment and the most important ones I have held true to my promise:

I will always be there, no matter where I am, for my heart and my soul are with you always.

I will never forget that moment, and the love and protective urge I felt towards you, nor my vow that I would give my life to protect you.

I will always do my best to be a man that you could respect, a friend you could trust, and a Father you could sincerely love.

I will treat you as the gift of God that you are, and respect the high honor that He has entrusted me with for your care.

I will love you 'til the day I die, but even then, I will leave behind a blanket of memories that will warm you until you open your beautiful eyes and smile at me once again!

A Song for a Godly Woman

May your life be like a praise song,

with each day a note on the keys;

and let each note you sing be lifelong;

filled with melody, joy and peace.

Let the chords resound in splendor,

and let your music soar

to rise before the Living God,

to bless Him with your score!

May your song be bold yet humble,

as it gives our God His praise;

and may He bless your life in return

with full and abundant days!

And when the strings are quiet

and the notes have worked their peace,

ay your song be seen as beautiful,

like a rose upon the Keys.

All Along the Way

Through all the years

Above all the tears

Over all the miles

Beyond all the smiles

More than words can say

I have loved my precious gift of God

All along the way!

The Lilies Will Bloom Again

Some things we can be sure of,

Those things that never change;

That spring will follow winter's chill

And the lilies will bloom again;

That time will pass and we'll grow old

And our babies become mothers;

That families that take time to care

Are precious to each other;

That God is Master of all things,

And His Holy Word is true;

That we should love those He sends to love

As Jesus commands that we do.

A Note for My Daughter on Her 21st Birthday

As sunrise moves unceasingly towards the sunset, it leaves in its wake a day to be filled. A day that will never come again; for each day is unique unto itself; filled with promise; swollen with potential; precariously poised to be lifted to God as a well stewarded gift, or toppled and spilled shamefully at His feet.

My prayer for you is that you find your peace in each moment filled; that your prayers are lifted on sturdy wings, and land in the bosom of God; that your heart be filled with joy, even in those times that you feel you couldn't ever smile again. May you be filled with the power to climb every mountain; and may you be nurtured by the faith that He will catch you if you fall. May your dreams all come true; may the joy of your children's laughter ring all around you; and may your children's, children's, children present their children to you for a blessing. May you have the mate who has been defined in the prayers of your parents, and ancestors before them; may he love you as much as we who hold you so special in our hearts; and may your heart beat with love for him.

You are a woman now. Find a dream to define in your heart, set your sights on the mark, and daily move towards it. You have a wonderful life before you; seize each moment and let your life be as the sea: through ebbs and flows, through storms and calm, and heat and cold; it always reflects the Son.

Balloon Bouquets

Light and carefree and dancing towards the light.

Joyful and colorful; it is such a gorgeous sight.

Waving and bouncing; so innocent and pure

It moves in freedom, though connected and secure.

It searches for its limits, as it reaches to the sky.

And constantly adjusts its path to breezes passing by.

May your life's blessings mimic that balloon bouquet,

May you be blessed with peace at the end of every day.

May your joys be many and may your troubles be few,

May you dance on gentle breezes, as God pours His grace on you!

Transitions – Daughter

So much of the success we have in life depends on how well we handle the necessary transitions that the Lord allows in our lives to challenge us; that embrace greater opportunities and responsibilities.

Many are afraid to face the storms that come with transitions. They cower, even though the Master has promised to calm their stormy seas.

We are admired if we handle transitions without losing connection. Facing the storms; wise enough to grab the umbrella and courageous enough not to let the threatening clouds keep us indoors.

The key point in dealing with transition is in knowing that we go through them.

They don't stop coming.

The wise welcome them.

They lead us to better places!

Enter into each transition with tremendous hope, immense faith, and a heart filled with joy!

Your Essence is Beautiful

For My Granddaughter, Jacylah, at 3

Many years from now, when you look back at being three, I hope you will be looking back over many years of pleasant memories as you reminisce this particular time in your life.

I pray that it is God's will that we who love you can run far with you. But, whenever we take a different fork in life's road, I pray that you will always feel our presence as you travel toward the purpose for which you were called.

I hope that our love for you and our hopes for you are an encouragement, but that the love of God and your hopes in His promise are what truly feed your sense of well being.

I hope that you are always surrounded, as you are today, by those who adore you. I hope they recognize you for the princess that you are: not so much because you are so pretty, but because your very essence is beautiful.

A Wedding Prayer for Mika

May Love, joy, peace, and happiness,
And health, and wealth, and great success
Fill your lives with His blessedness.
May your love stay vibrant and true.
May you honor each other in all of your ways,
May your lives be filled with fruitful days
May you smile as you watch your children play
May they love and cherish you.
And let Jesus walk closely with you.
And when troubles come, and know that they will,
Just remember the Cross that stood on that hill
And the blood that was shed there delivers you still
When Jesus is walking with you.
And though dark days come, for come they must,
Remember the One in whom you put your trust,
And that with Him you have more than enough
When Jesus is walking with you.
May you live to see all your dreams come true
Not only your dreams but your children's too
May your triumphs be many and your troubles be few,
Just let Jesus walk closely with you.
When your bodies grow old and your heads have turned gray
And most of us here have long gone our way
Remember this song and recall that I prayed

That the words of this song come true

That through all those years,

Through your hopes and your fears

That your love always felt like new

And that two lives that were wedded together

Grew in grace and got better and better

Because Jesus was walking with you.

May Love, joy, peace, and happiness,

And health, and wealth, and great success

Fill your lives with His blessedness.

May your love stay vibrant and true.

But much more than this,

My deepest wish is that Jesus walks always with you.

On Her First Mothers' Day

Was not so very long ago, you sat upon my knee.

All toothless smiles, and big bright eyes, as cute as you could be.

I watched you grow not long ago into a beautiful young lady,

And though you are a woman now, you'll always be my baby.

And now my baby girl is a mother, with a baby on her knee,

All toothless smiles, and big bright eyes, you're proud as you can be!

You'll watch him grow, the time will fly; months give way to years.

The prayers you lift for the man he'll be, will help subdue your fears.

He'll let you know, by word and deed, in every way he can

That he loves you for the love you gave, as he became a man.

That's the same way Jesus loves you; more than words can say.

May the joy and peace that His love brings, warm your heart each day.

A Letter from My Daughter

On the Occasion of My 52nd Birthday

My Dearest Father,

It seems that as I grow older, I appreciate more and more how wonderful a father you are. There are so many things, growing up, that I can't remember. However, one memory remains constant; and that is how much you adored me. You showed me from the beginning of my life how it should feel to be loved, respected, cherished, and revered. You always took the time to listen to me. You understood me better than I understood myself. You connected with me in a way that no one ever has or will again. We can have conversations without saying a word to one another. You can always sense when something is going on with me, even though you are miles away. For these things I am eternally grateful.

You taught me how important it is to have peace in your life. To always seek God's face; not only in the midst of a storm, but also when things are going just right. You taught me that mistakes are life lessons and not failures. You taught me that it is better to have loved and lost than never to have loved at all. You taught me patience. You taught me how to laugh. Seems silly, but even at a young age you kept me laughing. And, even now, I use laughter as a healing method; not only for myself, but for others around me as well. You taught me about priorities and how important it is to keep them in line. You taught me how to let things go and let God. For these things I am abundantly blessed.

You embedded into my mind what a true man of God should be; what it should feel like to be loved. You set the perfect example of the kind of man I want to father my children, because you are such a wonderful father. Though in years past I have made some awful decisions regarding who I would allow into my heart, I always knew that whoever I wound up with would have to be a lot like you.

Dad, you are the center of my joy. Your smile brightens my world. Your quiet, caring ways make me feel like I am a princess, every day. I am so richly blessed to have you in my life. I realize now, just how rare it is these days to have a wonderful healthy relationship with your father. But I do! You are constantly in my thought s and prayers, and I know that the same holds true for you.

I adore you. I respect you. I cherish you. I admire you. I love you. I miss you. Thank you for being such a wonderful father. Thank you for teaching me so many valuable life lessons that I see coming into play as I grow older. Thank you for always putting me and Trevor first in your life. Thank you for allowing me to experience what it is, and should be, like to be #1 in someone's life. Thank you for keeping all of your promises. Thank you for never judging me, but for keeping your love for me constant, regardless of my mistakes. Thank you for showing me Jesus, just by being you. Thank you for giving me so many wonderful childhood memories. Thank you for building castles in the sand with me. Thank you for taking me on all those long bike rides. Thank you for Shadrach (my childhood dog). Thank you for letting me stay up late with you to spend quality time. Thank you for singing to me at night. Thank you for going to all of my games and pageants. Thank you for driving miles and miles when you were working and living in Connecticut just to be able to tuck me in and make breakfast in the morning only to turn around to go right back to work. Thank you for never complaining. Thank you for protecting me. Thank you for praying for me. Thank you for always supporting and encouraging me. Thank you for loving me. Thank you for not only being my father, but for being my 'Daddy' too!

For all these things, and so many more,

I Love You!

I always have and I always will.

Good Daddies

As beautiful as a wispy cloud stained golden by the setting sun ,
As warm as a blush, and as gentle as a summer breeze.

Giggling like a mountain stream dancing over smooth rocks, and
frolicking like a butterfly exploring a blue buddleias.

As curious as a kitten and as protective as a momma grizzly.

Craving attention like a collie pup and even more huggable.

Delicate as a crystal goblet and as adaptable as the shoreline to
ever changing tides.

How naturally they receive the love and wisdom we pour into
them; our beautiful daughters.

How unfortunate the man who runs from the immense joy of
guiding and protecting her into womanhood.

How impoverished is the man who has never had her draw his
image and entitle her masterpiece; "My Daddy" in crayon.

Despicable is the man who confuses correction and abuse,
chastisement and degradation, affection and depravity.

Blessed is the man that cherishes the honor of being a Good
Daddy to this precious gift from God.

She will honor you in her being, and your grandchildren will
speak of you in terms that honor your name.

Love with Certainty

Love; a word we use so capriciously. We say it about things: "I love sunny days." We say it about words; "I love that idea." We say it about our cars, our homes, our favorite vacation spots, our favorite foods, our friends, our fellow man, our family, our children, our mates, and our God. If we take a look at how we feel about any of the above, we have to admit that we feel differently about the "love" we have for each of them. The Greeks use five words to better define the types of love being expressed: *Mania* (obsessive desire to possess), *Eros* (emotional, heated, desire to be with intimately), *Philos* (love towards a friend or relative), *Storgy* ('motherly love', parent/child love, based on dependency), and *Agapeo* (unconditional love from one party to another).

I created a term for this section; Love with Certainty. It is that love that often begins as Eros and grows into Philos (or vice versa), that grows to blend with a measure of Agape. It is the stuff that makes us fall in love and want to stay in love. It is the type of love that makes us smile when we see the other coming our way. It is the love that makes it feel like holding them close is the natural thing to do. It is the kind of love that drives us to think of ways to bring happiness into their lives. It is the kind of love that makes us wish we could carry all of their troubles and ease all of their pain. It is the type of love that inspires us to put their desires and needs before our own. It is the type of love that drives us to seek time to be alone with them when words are welcome but not necessary; a touch is not needed but highly desired. It is the love a loving husband has for his loving wife. Mania and Storgy are not welcomed in this mix, because they can pollute the blend. I pray that the words I have written to my wife will inspire those who fear drinking from this intoxicating cup to sip expectantly, drink deeply, and savor the sweetness of its nectar. I pray that when you decide to, that you love with certainty.

Spring

Earth lies back to watch the Sun

She craves the warmth of his caress.

Never free of her lustful gaze, he starts his dance;

The snows are melting, the nights grow short.

"Yes My Love do come to me" she moans.

She softens to the magic of his song.

"Give yourself in truth to me;

Let me warm your bed.

I will remove the death of the frost and

I will arouse you to the flame that is life.

My Love, I will touch your mountains here;

See the snows melt into the river's flows?

And I will caress your valleys here,

Feel the singing of your greening song!

Precious, I will blow on your meadows here;

Hear how I make your flowers grow?

Now, I will kiss your forest there;

Smell how I make your sap run free!

Quake Earth Quake and rejoice: for I have made you flow;

And I have made you sing: I have made you blossom;

I have made you mine: and yet I've set you free!

For we have made a child named Spring;

And Spring forever will make Love!

Behold My Beloved

Look into the mirror clear and

Behold my beloved staring back at you;

But linger not too long within her eyes

For there in those pools of caramel brown

Swim inducements and enticements

But nothing there for quenching the thirst

No Matter how long you might linger and drink.

Behind those eyes lies the mind fed by the soul

That dances with the spirit that loves me.

Sometimes in silence that loudly proclaims peace;

Sometimes in laughter that dances in the confidence of hope;

But always in the immutable presence of love.

Behold the one who rejoices most in my existence,

And the one who will be most empty when I am gone,

Whose eyes I will sorely miss if they close before mine.

Smile back at her smiling with perfect lips and let her know

Your heart dances with joy because you behold my beloved!

Now

I have danced in the fog of the madness of love, before.

My days seemed endless and my nights too brief before.

The one who understood me grew to misunderstand me, before.

I've lived without the one I couldn't live without, before.

I am dancing in the warm peaceful rays of the topaz sunset, now.

My days are full and swift and the nights long and restful, now.

I am known; well known and accepted for what I am, now.

I will live with the one I cannot live without in Christ, forever.

Love at the Feet of God

The Rose is pampered by the sunshine, but it is nurtured by the rain.....and so is love!

If love were not challenged by the circumstances of life, how then would we come to appreciate the comfort it brings against their effects?

Love is not diminished by circumstance, neither is it dismayed. It does not consider itself a stone, but, rather, a feather that floats on the wings of faith and lands softly at the feet of God.

Blessed

We're all blessed in different ways
With blessings from above.
Some with health, some with wealth
And some of us with love.
Health and wealth have their appeal.
And all of that is fine.
But I know that I am greatly blessed,
Because my love is mine!

Coming Home to Peace

Peace comes from knowing that there is a someplace
Where fear has no name and scorn has no address.
A place where peace gives rise to comfort;
And comfort to contentment and contentment to rest;
A place to rest my head and bury my face in warm flesh;
A place where I am not only welcomed but desired;
A place where love flows from the depths of our being;
A place designed to buffer against the world.
A place where passion tutors reason.
It is here that passions are fueled,
And we yield to the joy of our peace.
In our passion we fear neither ecstasy nor tears,
For whatever we share is to be cherished.

The Truth About Marshmallows

Thank God for marshmallows. They grumble while reaching in their pockets to fill needs both identified and discerned. They always let those they love learn by standing on their own two feet while leaning strongly against their backs to make sure that they don't fall.

They won't put up with that anymore...today! Ten minutes after chewing you out they are there licking your wounds. Always driving too fast to stop, but slamming on the brakes at just the right moment.

Never forgetting yet always forgiving because the rest of our lives begins right now.

May my favorite marshmallow be abundantly blessed just as she has been such an abundant blessing.

With Certainty

What assurance allows expectations of a smile when you see me?

How audacious is presumption that my voice is your music?

How bold am I to reach for your hand; not fearing your reaction?

Can the impertinence of my intimate conversation be tolerated?

With what certainty do I assume that you welcome my embrace?

Just how brazen am I that I would reach for you at sunrise?

Is it because I learned that your smile always greets mine?

Perhaps it is only a courteous gesture in response to my smile.

Then deep must be the well from which you draw inspiration,

For the smile I give to you is unencumbered by anything but joy!

It would seem that sometimes indicates obligatory routine,

But always is the platter upon which heartfelt joy is served.

I notice that your eyes dance whenever we speak face to face.

So too does your voice when I am exiled from those lovely orbs.

As if drawn to the bandstand, you turn to me whenever I speak,

And courteously tolerate my inanities to search for reason.

When I speak low, you speak low. When I laugh, you laugh.

When I moan, you moan. It's like my melody drives your lyric.

I remember wondering how wonderful it would be. Now I know.

I know just how delicately warm and soft and silky smooth it is.

That hand that I so longed to hold is the frontier of my desires.

Like your lovely face and your beautiful eyes your hand is free;

Exposed to any eye drawn by chance or appreciation of beauty.

But only my hand enwraps it in knowing and feels welcomed.

What things I speak to those delicate ears cause my cheeks to flush.

Not that they are lewd, for our minds are as undefiled as our bed;

It is just that whatever bonds I can imagine, I paint with my tongue.

No words are beyond boundaries if they draw us closer.

My words caress you and soothe you and calm you and...

You do not rebuke them nor bruise them nor turn them away.

Like a supple willow yields to the advances of the summer breeze,

So do I feel your warm and lovely body succumb to my

embrace.

You welcome me and pour yourself against me to destroy distance.

So close that our necks must crane to melt our smiles into kisses.

Heat flows from you like fever and you tremble, but not from fear.

My assumptions are validated when tenderly I reach for you.

With certainty I know you will not recoil when I caress you at dawn.

My certainty is born on the remembrance of a thousand sultry nights

Awakening into bright balmy days of my loving you with certainty.

Dee's Are What I Wish for You

I pray that you never lose your Desire as lovers;

That you not only want each other but crave each other;

Not sought or quenched under a stranger's cover,

 All the days of your lives.

That you Delight in your closeness; each moment enchanted

That the joy that you share not be taken for granted

Cherish each other's presence, but never demand it,

 All the days of your lives.

That you Decide to be joyful and faithful in love;

Not based on emotions but strength from above;

That you honor in truth, the vows you spoke of,

All the days of your lives.

That you Devote your all to nurture your marriage.

And to the blessing of children He puts in your carriage,

And esteem for your union may you never disparage

All the days of your lives.

I pray that you Dedicate your family to serving

To honor The Lord, neither halting nor swerving

And be blessed that God finds your service deserving.

All the days of your lives.

Understand that the Discipline of love is immutable.

Love is a decision that stands on a vow indisputable.

If you stand together on the Rock that's immovable,

All the days of your lives.

Above All Else

Love is timeless and boundless.
Love is gentle and love is kind.
Love is warm and love is sweet.
Love carries the scent of roses,
caresses like a summer breeze,
and soothes like a gentle rain!
Love sings songs and whispers!
It writes letters that melt hearts.
It is sparkling wine and
strawberries and candlelight.
Love floats like goose down.
And soars like an eagle in pursuit.
Love basks like a cat in sunlight,
And frolics like puppies in tall grass.
Love's call is primal like an alpha wolf
And protects like a she bear in May.
Love is steamy and love is hot.
Love is neither a weakness
Nor a strength that makes us weak.
Love is mysterious, yet it enlightens.
Love seeks peace and avoids strife.
It neither walks in fear nor in malice.
Love is commanded but never demanding.
Love is patient and deferential.
Love is pure and love is sacred.
Love is of God; for God is Love.
True love is faithful and everlasting,
and above all else,
Love fights to endure all things!

In Remembrance

I remember the last day I spent with my mother. It was a big family weekend: Christmas party on Saturday and my sister's annual charity banquet on Sunday. She was so full of laughter, and peacemaking, and encouragement, and kindness, and love. How beautiful it was to be her family at Christmas time. At any time really, but Christmas was the time of the year that she shined even more brightly.

How could I know when I hugged her and kissed her good-bye that day, that it would be the last embrace, the last kiss, the last knowing nod, the last good-bye? Within the week, so many were expressing love and support during our hour of sorrow.

There was nothing left unsaid between us. I am not unveiling any depths of feeling or admiration or thankfulness now that I had not expressed to her in life. Thanks be to Jesus that I had the opportunity, from 500 miles away, to tell her I loved her, one more time, within the hour that she took her last breath; at a moment when we were optimistically looking forward to the next UConn basketball game, and Christmas, less than 5 days away.

Life is fragile and very precious, and with great care and tenderness should we treat those lives God has placed within our influence to uphold, protect, and encourage. Those of you who still have your mothers and fathers and grandmothers and grandfathers and aunts and uncles with you, give them an extra measure of love and attention. It will be a gift to them far more precious than anything you could wrap in pretty paper. And if they are no longer here, honor them by honoring their husbands or wives, or fathers or mothers or sisters or brothers or children or grandchildren. Leave no words of love unexpressed or acts of kindness left in a basket of promises.

Unfortunately, life will provide a season for all of us to someday experience this peculiar brand of sadness. Hopefully, when that time comes, you will not be found regretting that which you did not say; that which you did not do; but rather rejoicing that you loved them as best you could and poured out that love in thought, word, and deed.

Time tries all things. Now fades to then. Today serves its purpose and turns to slip away with yesterday on its shadowy journey. Even tomorrow visits only for a moment in its headlong race to that place in time that is too long ago to remember.

Our babies become elders who keep us alive only in the elusive, memories they convey and the faded photos they serve like so many sugar cookies on a silver tray. Nothing stays the same. Mountain peaks will one day crumble into sand dunes and raging rivers will become nothing more than stains on the rocks they polish as smooth as jewels.

Yet it is important that we remember "those times" that are anchors to our pasts that refrain the ship of time from breaking free and dashing madly into the future without connection to the navigational skills that come from all those things that "those times" taught us.

My prayer is that this section will spark a recollection of a pleasant place in your memories, or inspire you to value the people, places, and pleasures we too often take for granted.

Today is That Tomorrow

I fear that today is that tomorrow that I dreaded yesterday

When I'd look back, and mourn the days that I let slip away.

It seemed like there was so much time. This day seemed so
distant,

But I could not restrain those days. They fled me in an instant.

So I warn those just starting out on the road to the setting sun,

Value each moment; cherish each day and work to squander none.

Time like sand in a tight clenched hand will too soon slip away.

And I pray when your tomorrows come, that you not mourn your
yesterdays.

Save Me a Spot My Brother

(A Tribute to Albert Louis Reaves, Jr.)

Save me a spot my brother, as you stand there by the shore

By the riverside at the even tide, free from pain forevermore

Save me a spot my brother where calm breezes speak of peace

Where joy is everlasting and where all your troubles cease

Save me a spot my brother, 'til I too have made my rod

Of all of life's joys and trials while trusting in my God

'Til I fill that spot my brother, I'll stand by memories' pool

And smile again, and keep reeling in precious thoughts of you.

The Reunion

They stood on the raft of life in the midst of the river of time and called out to us, all of us, even those who were yet unborn. It is to us that they traveled and it is for us that they weathered the stormy seas that bridge the distance between the craggy shores of despair and the soft sun kissed beaches of promise.

Because of us, they bound their rafts together, so that through the many of their bonds, strengthened by the ties of their shared blood heritage, they could make a place for us to be born into love and nurtured by knowing who we are, and where we are from, and where their dreams would land us on that beauteous beach of hope.

Their prayers were lifted to the Father above that this day would come. That this day of reunion and days like it that have already past, and all those that are yet to come, would serve to strengthen the bonds that would never come undone. They prayed that as their generation meandered with certainty into the glories of the sunset, that my generation would stand strong in their stead, as we approach the twilight of our years, and call to our children, and they to theirs, and to those yet unknown to never cut the bindings, never lose the caring, never lose the pride in knowing from whence we came, and to whom we are attached.

Soon this raft will fall apart. I can feel it. The river of time decays its beams and loosens its lasts, but while yet afloat, I think of you, and hope for you, and pray for you.

And when this raft too has fallen apart (as will yours one day), like so many others who journey with me, and those that have gone before me, I know I will be swept away to that place where the sunset kisses the horizon of the boundless river of time, and there be laid to rest gently on the shore of promise of my Father.

There will be nothing you can do but remember, but isn't that the very essence of the continuance of life? I simply ask that you remember well. Remember that those who came before you prayed that you would stay together in love, and gain from that union all that is the best part of your family ties. Teach your children of the bonds they share, one with the other; teach them of the power they have in the oneness of their kindred spirits; teach them that they are worthy of each other's love and that love is at the heart of understanding their true meaning as instruments of God; for it is in sharing His love for us, with each other, that we truly fulfill the dreams of our fathers; the hopes of our mothers; and the calling and purpose of God for our lives.

As we travel down the river of time, sometimes, along the way, we are blessed to find companions to share those trying miles, and much more sweet is that journey when we share bonds that neither time nor circumstance can break. After we have shared the distances filled with countless longings fueled by hope filled dreams, and poured out efforts to overcome the turbulence that so often besets us, by standing on our faith stained with our sweat and blood, and succumbed to passions pregnant with contagious laughter and hidden tears, the journey must eventually end. It is often not until then that we can appreciate that the rhythm of the paddling of our companions' oars has transcended the distance between us, and that we have sailed in unity. Even after the river has forked, and the sounds of that familiar paddling grows faint down the river of time, those companions fill a place of friendship through kinship, nurtured by our common bonds, and travel forever on the flowing streams of our wandering memories. From that place, neither time nor space can erase the remembrance of those seasons when we shared the joys of our youth.

Our time of reunion is a time to create new memories and to indelibly burn the images in our minds of those family members and friends who have never held a place in our mind's eye before; a time to meet the children of our kinship for whom we pray in anonymity; a time to plan closer walks for some of us; a time to unknowingly say our last good-byes for others of us.

Our time of reunion is a time to reclaim the fragrance of those seasons that have lodged themselves so indelibly in our memories. It is a time to reach into the wine cellars of our minds and find the choicest vintage; dust it off, open it up, and savor the aroma of its fine bouquet. Like a fine wine, our memories are fermented in the charred kegs of our hearts, to be poured out and shared at times of celebration. It is often then that a mere sip from that fluted glass can refresh our very souls; but unlike fine wine, our memories can be shared and sipped upon frequently, without ever fearing that the bottle will run dry.

I rejoice in seeing you again, and in meeting those who come behind you, and pray that we will meet yet again. Until we do, but even if we cannot, we can go to the wine cellar and select from the vintage we trod together, and sip, and taste those precious moments once again.

May the Lord bless your life in all the most important ways. May He protect and nurture you all the days of your life; and if He allows that we meet again, let us remember when we rowed that common stream, and know that a common blood, powered by a common heartbeat, transcends the distances between us. And when we stand on that shore of promise, our faces framed by that never setting sunset, may we rejoice in our being forever together.

Bridges

I crossed so many bridges

I climbed mountains

I walked meadows

I sojourned valleys

I navigated rugged terrain

I skirted rivers

I jumped brooks

And I crossed so many bridges

Bridges helped me

Traverse caverns deep

Ravines steep

Rivers raging

Bridges helped me

Avoid obstacles insurmountable

Routes redirected

Time delayed

Bridges helped me

When I was confused

Without options

Feeling weak

Bridges helped me

To cross over

Stand above

Get beyond

Bridges helped me

In my longest days

Darkest Hours

Weakest moments

Bridges helped me

To ease the pain

My mind

The way

Bridges helped me

By providing tremendous inspiration

Immense hope

Great joy

Bridges helped me

Learn to embrace change

Maintain faith

Cherish love

Bridges helped me

But now some are forever gone

Reverently cherished

Sorely missed

My journey was very long

Sometimes dangerous

Often surprising

Rarely smooth

Constantly changing

Frequently blocked

Always perplexing

My journey was long but never hopeless

Thank You Lord for sending me sturdy bridges
Thank You Lord for shoring my bridges
Thank You Lord for being a bridge
Thank You Lord for making me a bridge
Thank You Lord for blessing those yet to cross this bridge

Whitney Died Yesterday

Songbird, fly away; fly back to glorious days.

When you sang before the Lord and He blessed you

When you sang for joy and only He possessed you.

Fly there again. Leave this trial behind you,

Where there is always something there to remind you

That today is not as promised on yesterday

And the tomorrows of your hope have danced away.

Though quiet now, your song still rings

From everywhere we hear you singing;

Your voice in the beauty of the best of you;

As we promise to not speak of what became of you,

Or bemoan it's such a shame, what happened to you;

How you died unfulfilled; seeking the irreplaceable;

How we had longed the return of your better days.

But this is not our show. We can't call songbirds to sing.

It is God's will that is fulfilled, but we will learn from this.

You will return to the place of your first song; to the One for

Whom you were singing.

Though we mourn you on earth, they stand in heaven cheering;

Rejoicing in He Who brought you safely home, and she who is

now home singing.

Then I Can Rest in Peace

Lord, You have given me this precious gift, to encourage in Your name;
To soothe souls stained by sin and guilt and scarred by fear and shame.
So if I can show someone Your face
And help someone to know Your grace
And encourage them to run this race,
Then I can rest in peace.

This gift that You have given me is not for me to hide
But for every soul that it allures to Your precious bleeding side.
And if there someone receives Your love
That frees them by Your cleansing blood
That saves them from sin's deadly flood
Then I can rest in peace.

So fill my mind and guide my heart to do as You have called
To raise a hallowed banner high, that crowns You Lord of All.
If I help someone to see your ways
By telling them what your Word says
That there is hope because Jesus saves,
Then I can rest in peace.

And when my race is over, and You have called me to my rest
I pray the words I leave behind, pass time's most crucial test.
May my words live to speak of Thee,
To the children of my progeny,
Make their joy in You my legacy,
Then I can rest in peace.

My Big Green Book

Time stands still in my big green book
Filled with love and all the time it took
To assemble my awards and words of praise
With pictures and clippings from yesterdays.
Memories I am glad that my mother kept
Because I was too busy at being adept
At those things she so proudly memorialized,
Her hero viewed through timeless eyes.
Oh how I cherish my big green book,
But more the woman whose love it took.
When my grandchildren see it, I hope they think of,
Not about what I did, but how great was her love!

My Last Breath

If I knew I would not witness the setting of my next sunrise,
Nor the rising of its moon, what would I long for?
I simply pray that my last breath not be empty.
That it be a grunt rather than a whimper.
That it not regret words yet unspoken, nor acts left undone,
Nor talents unused, nor dreams unsought,
Nor warnings unheeded, nor my calling unanswered;
That it not be unrepentant, and that it not be unappreciative.
Neither let it be unheard, nor, not mourned.
Above all, I pray that it blesses the name of Jesus,
And joyfully announces my arrival into His presence!

About the Author

Chuck Goode was born in Hartford, CT, in 1949, into a working class family that put great value on the importance of bringing honor to God and family. His childhood was marked by the conflicts of trying to excel in a neighborhood that was more focused on the physical prowess of a young man than the intellectual. He was successful as he learned to purge bad influences and gain favor with those he respected. Influenced by Rudyard Kipling's poem "If", he learned to 'walk with kings…' yet never lost '…the common touch.' Chuck showed skills in art and poetry at an early age. His first published poem, "Books", was a prize winner in a national poetry contest, but he never saw it again after it was published.

An excellent student and athlete, he received scholarship offers from some of the best universities in the country, but the one he cherished and honored was from his beloved state university; UConn. A serious knee injury in his sophomore year, allowed him only sporadic practice time during his junior and senior campaigns, but he started every game and performed admirably. He carried that same competitive spirit and tenacity into his life after graduation. Over the years, as his relationship with God grew, his writing became more inspired by revelations from The Spirit, and his deep love for his family. Most of his work involves Godly encouragement, and many of his works were birthed in creating greeting cards and tributes for his family.

After his retirement from a career as a sales manager, in 2011, he began his own publishing company, Goode God Publishing. "Whispers Just Before Dawn" is the first book published by the company. A major historical novel is in the final stages and the expected publishing date is in 2014.

Index